The
Resilience Club

Daily success habits of
long-term high performers

Angela Armstrong PhD

RETHINK PRESS

First published in Great Britain in 2019 by Rethink Press
(www.rethinkpress.com)

Praise for *The Resilience Club*

'The world belongs to the resilient. Join *The Resilience Club* to multiply purposeful energy in yourself and all those you touch.'

Kevin Cashman,
Global Leader of CEO & Executive Development,
Korn Ferry, bestselling author of *Leadership from the Inside Out* and *The Pause Principle*

'In today's fast-paced working environment, resilience is a critical skill set for all leaders to master. Angela walks-her-talk on resilience and incorporated the topic into the strategic leadership programme she designed and delivers for us. *The Resilience Club* is an essential and practical guide for those seeking to deliver high-quality, sustainable results.'

Tony Bickerstaff,
Chief Financial Officer, Costain Group PLC

'*The Resilience Club* is essential reading for busy entrepreneurs who want to be brave, have fun and make a positive impact in the world. It's packed with tried-and-tested habits to manage your time, energy and emotions so you have more capacity to get stuff done.'

Daniel Priestley,
CEO, Dent Global

'It's great to see a micro-learning approach in *The Resilience Club*. Having thirty habits is very reader-friendly for busy people. Angela has nailed it – specific small lifestyle changes that make a massive difference to your well-being and your results.'

Helen Routledge,
CEO, Totem Learning, author of
Why Games are Good for Business

'Investing in your personal resilience is the best career move you'll ever make. *The Resilience Club* shows you how.'

Debra Martin,
Partner, Geldards LLP

'If you are looking to shift the perception of well-being and resilience from something "fluffy" to a core part of driving excellence in performance, then Angela is your woman. She ably blends her own experiences with simply delivered concepts that we can all relate to. Her storytelling moves the dial for even the most sceptical people. I can personally vouch for the fact that Angela's FREEDOM model results in shifting what we *know* into what we actually *do*.'

Nic Heffernan,
Head of Corporate Projects, Coventry Building Society

'As a person, Angela exemplifies integrated leadership, skilfully blending deep compassion and care for the individual with a results-driven focus for the business. The habits in *The Resilience Club* provide a simple "how to" for you to do the same.'

Okokon Udo, PhD,
consultant, coach, speaker, professor and facilitator

'Today's workforce demands a lot from leaders: to be purpose-driven, authentic, inclusive, visionary yet humble; to create a space of psychological safety for their people; and to show up without the armour of hierarchy. These demands can create a significant emotional load on leaders who are facing into a tide of consumer and shareholder activism, disruptive change to business practices and endless cost focus. Now is the time to understand that working on our personal resilience is not a sign of weakness, but of strength. Packed with simple yet powerful tools to add to your toolkit, I believe *The Resilience Club* is a must-read practical guide for anyone feeling the pressure at work.'

Jaime Maxwell-Grant,
EMEA Digital Practice Lead, Korn Ferry

'*The Resilience Club* offers simple, powerful habits help you to stay healthy, sane and spirited in a demanding world.'

Carrie Caladine,
Owner and Managing Director, Right Legal Group

'You can immunise yourself against the rising tide of workplace stress by adopting these simple and powerful resilience habits. Having spent 30 years as a business leader, I recognise *The Resilience Club* as a valuable source of lessons learned that underpin sustainable high performance. I recommend it to anyone aspiring to be an authentic leader.'

Mike Byrne,
Managing Director, Birkdale Consultancy Limited

'Higher education is undergoing a period of significant change. Angela's insights and experience on change, leadership and resilience inspire and support us to continually deliver excellence. Developing proactive resilience practices is vital for staff and student well-being, and for student employability.'

Professor Kath Mitchell,
Vice-Chancellor, University of Derby

'Mental health is a current issue that both employer and employee need to work on. I've spent seventeen years in HR roles. Angela's insights and refreshing blend of being both bold and kind really works. I'm recommending *The Resilience Club* to everyone in a stretch role.'

Jenny Tomkins,
HR Operations Director, Costain Group PLC

'Leadership resilience should not be left to chance. *The Resilience Club* includes habits to help you develop clarity of purpose, vulnerability-based trust, adaptability and personal alignment.'

John D Anderson MBE,
Performance Director, British Canoeing 1997–2017

'Supporting people to improve their personal resilience is a hot topic for leaders across our global network. *The Resilience Club* offers practical solutions that are simple, fast and free.'

Jenni Waller,
Executive Director, Maximum Performance International

Contents

For leaders, change-makers and everyone who wants to get out of bed each day and give life their best shot.

Foreword

We are more technologically connected and more emotionally disconnected than ever before. Fast-paced change creates high workloads and considerable uncertainty, leading to stress and overwhelm. New products and services, technological advances, mergers and acquisitions, culture change, restructuring and redundancies are all the norm.

On a global scale, we face issues of climate change, artificial intelligence and the future of work, plastic in the oceans, rainforests being destroyed, political instability, social inequality, terrorist activity and more. The list is endless, and that's before you take into account the added personal pressures of children, education, health issues, caring for ageing parents and so on.

Exhausted yet? This is our daily reality.

The global nature of the issues we face is a fundamental shift in what it means to be human in the twenty-first century. We are tackling global economic and societal issues on a monumental scale in a global economy while dealing with local issues as well. Even the most resilient of people need to upskill to cope. Help is at hand, thanks to Dr Angela Armstrong. Welcome to *The Resilience Club*.

No matter how resilient or high performing you already are, Angela's book provides a guide to navigating the pressures of everyday life and work with more ease. I picked it up and breathed a sigh of relief. At last, here is a practical resource to remind you of some of the tools and techniques you may already know, and to introduce you to new ways of dealing with the stress and overwhelm that constant change and high workloads bring.

Angela and I each work with executive boards and senior leadership teams, we both see levels of stress and exhaustion rising to an almost crisis point. More worryingly, most leaders seem oblivious to the severity of the pressure they are under or how their exhaustion is negatively impacting productivity and behaviour in the workplace.

Many learn to cope by shutting down and numbing their emotions. This can result in leaders and teams disconnecting emotionally from themselves as well as each other, becoming transactional in interactions. What's worse is that you may not realise you are doing it. This is a real concern for the future of humanity as well as business.

When I first met Angela some years ago, she embodied the zest for life that is so often lacking in the workplace. Having read this book, I now understand why. She's equipped herself with coping mechanisms that enable her to sustain high performance and increase levels of connection while decreasing stress.

Angela is open about her personal journey of the pressure of leadership, burning out and bouncing back. This book is the culmination of years of research, daily practical application and feedback from clients, which she shares generously to help leaders upskill *before* they reach the crisis point of burnout.

Angela's FREEDOM model covers thirty habits to help reduce stress and create the capacity to take on new challenges. Some you can implement easily, others will take time and practice. These self-care habits provide powerful choices to enable you to perform at your optimum level over the long term. Packed full of useful tried-and-tested techniques, this is the definitive 'how to' reference book on developing personal resilience.

If we want a thriving business and society, we need more thriving leaders who have aliveness and human connection at the heart of their interactions.

Take the first step today and read this book. The world and humanity need you.

Jude Jennison,
Leadership advisor to executive teams
and author of the books *Leading through uncertainty*
and *Leadership beyond measure*

Introduction

Do you want to stay healthy, sane and spirited in a demanding world? Do you want to attain high performance *and* sustain it?

You are a capable, resourceful human being looking for support and direction to be the best you can be.

Research at the management consultants Korn Ferry, based on the largest database of leadership effectiveness in the world, demonstrates that *self-awareness* of top leadership is correlated with tangible, meaningful financial results. The data also shows that *purpose-driven* leadership drives engagement and performance and that *learning agility* is a greater predictor of potential than raw intellect. The habits in this book guide you to develop these qualities and many more. The habits are designed to challenge and support you to adapt your behaviour as a leader. By becoming a role model for self-care practices you will be able to think, act and behave from a place of being fully resourced. When you are fully resourced, you can have more influence and be a better colleague, friend, family and community member. It's not always easy, but it is worth it.

I am a leadership specialist, coach, trainer, speaker and business owner. In this book I share my actionable insights, informed by having had a significant career leading national transformation programmes in a global management consulting firm and returning to high performance following a period of burnout. Since 2010 I've built a strong track record of success delivering leadership training, executive coaching and learning consultancy to professional services firms (for example legal services, financial services, IT and consulting firms).

This book draws on up-to-date research, conversations with senior executives and my experience of working with individuals and teams to significantly improve their leadership performance and their quality of life. I have included case studies throughout the book illustrating the common outcomes of creating significantly more time, achieving promotion, increasing influence, creating emotional connections, being able to switch off and having abundant energy.

If you're already performing, and you want to sustain high performance long term, then this book was written for you. It is a practical, relevant and realistic 'how-to' reference book with additional learning resources available at www .TheResilienceClub.co.uk to extend the learning. I'm not going to cover the foundations of energy such as sleep, hydration, nutrition and movement, but there are books I recommend in Useful References.

What is resilience?

I define resilience as the ability to take the challenges and changes of life in your stride and say yes to the opportunities that excite you.

Proactively building our resilience habits can increase our capacity to take on more challenges, reduce existing stress and prepare ourselves for unexpected adversity. Typical challenges include family or relationship problems, health problems and workplace or financial stressors. Nine in ten of us will experience at least one traumatic event during our lives; for example, violent crime, a serious car accident, the sudden death of a loved one, a debilitating disease or a natural disaster. Challenges and changes can throw our lives into turmoil in unpredictable ways; no two people will respond to them in exactly the same way.

Stress is a choice

I first heard the phrase *stress is a choice* after I had burned out; in my denial I ranted at my occupational health counsellor. I came to realise that this one belief changed everything; it is the key to sustainable high performance and a life well lived.

By the time you've finished reading you will know:

- What currently triggers your stress response
- That what triggers stress is not always within your control, but how you perceive the trigger, and the way you respond to the trigger is
- Why you sometimes feel hijacked by stress hormones, and how you can take back control to experience the freedom that comes with emotional self-management
- The long-term effects of stress on your body
- Why talking about stress creates more stress! Talk about resilience instead

How to balance pressure, performance and renewal

Workplace stress has reached epidemic proportions. In Great Britain a staggering 595,000 workers suffered from work-related stress, depression or anxiety (Labour Force Survey 2018) – that's 1,800 per 100,000 employees who are members of the stress club. At the same time many people are succeeding in their careers and also have a fabulous quality of life away from the office, people who have learned the art of balancing pressure, performance and renewal – members of the Resilience Club.

In this section you will learn:

- Why sustainable high performance is better for business, and better for you
- How you personally define comfort, stretch and panic zones

- How you can sustain high levels of performance long term
- Why constant striving makes you less effective
- How to multiply the positive impact of fifteen minutes of rest

The FREEDOM model

You are naturally creative, resourceful and *whole*. You are not two half-beings that separately inhabit your work and life existence, yet many people act as if that's true. The FREEDOM model of resilience includes habits that help you invest in yourself as a whole person: mind, body, spirit and emotions.

By the time you've finished reading you will know:

- The power of being *whole*
- Where you already have good coping strategies, and where you can improve

This book is not about showing you how to 'suck it up' in a toxic situation. It is about helping you to step back and decide whether you want to have a different experience of your current role, help influence a culture change, or plot your exit to a company that actively supports employee well-being.

The resilience habits

The main part of the book is designed to be a reference guide that you can dip into as the need arises. Each of the habits follows the same pattern: what it is, why it is important, how to do it, benefits for you, benefits for others and related habits.

Most importantly, the habits are entirely within your control, simple to understand, quick to do, can be done anywhere, cost no money and require no kit.

This book contains habits in the following seven categories:

- **Focus** – How to manage workload demands to create the time to invest in your resilience. The discipline of directing your full attention to the one thing, within your control, that will move you forward fastest and help avoid overwhelm.

- **Role-models** – Create hope: if you can see it, you can be it. Curate a high-quality network to inspire your best so you can be a resilient leader who inspires others.

- **Energy** – Create, conserve and direct your energy: stay healthy, deliver maximum value and increase your influence.

- **Emotion** – Master your emotions: learn to let go of hurt, lean in to vulnerability, escape a vicious cycle and surf the emotional change curve like a pro.

- **Downtime** – Experience joy: learn to calm your mind, rest, play and get back to being you so you can experience more magic moments in life.

- **Optimism** – Believe: 'whatever happens, I will be alright'. Build confidence in your resourcefulness, bite off what you can chew to succeed, and direct your own path.

- **Meaning** – Why you do what you do: what we give meaning to influences our inner critic, allows us to dig deep, learn from failure, and have impact beyond ourselves.

The idea is to develop a balance of resilience habits across the seven categories – not mastery in each individual category. That way you'll have a broad range of coping strategies to handle a variety of challenges and opportunities that arise. There's a self-assessment exercise – the Wheel of Resilience exercises – in The FREEDOM Model chapter, or you can scan the habits and see what resonates.

Intentional practice

Sustainable high performers are not born; they are self-made through intentional resilience practice. Wherever you are on your leadership journey, now is always a good time to take proactive action to build your resilience – luck is when opportunity meets preparation. Whether you read this book cover to cover, or dip in to the bit that looks most interesting, take just 15 minutes to read something – and then put it into practice. Your future self will thank you.

Why I wrote this book

In 2010, in the wake of the global financial crisis, I had a massive wake-up call that the lifestyle I had been leading was no longer sustainable. Early one morning, getting ready for work, I had excruciating pain in my chest and thought I was going to die. I was 38, and in the prime of my career. At that time, I was leading national and global transformational change programmes. I worked for a huge management consulting firm that was known for high performance. I had won awards and was ranked in the top 5% of performance for my peer group. I had a full life outside of work too, and I was planning my wedding.

That day everything changed. I burned out. I suffered a physical and mental collapse due to workplace stress. One day I was in work, the next day I was an exhausted shell unable to do anything but sleep and basic self-care. I ended up having three months off work and then a three-month phased return to work. Those were the loneliest and most scary months of my life. My road back to full health was an education in health and well-being, mindset and emotional mastery. I developed lifestyle habits and workplace practices that, I believe, can literally save lives. Looking back, I am deeply grateful for my burnout, it woke me up and invited me to play a much bigger game, to achieve something beyond myself. I found my purpose.

Three years after that pivotal moment, I left my corporate job to start my own leadership-development firm working with clients in professional services. Since 2013 I have been working with senior leaders to create a culture of sustainable high performance. Not too long ago, leaders took time to engage with their people when demands were light, and at other times were expected to demonstrate a degree of stoicism – 'get over it and get on with it'. Today's leaders continue to navigate demands from a broad range of stakeholders, organisational changes and ongoing financial pressures. But now leaders are also expected to demonstrate a high level of emotional self-mastery because employees want leaders to be purpose-driven, accessible, inspiring, personable and inclusive. There is a greater expectancy for openness, transparency, vulnerability *and* courage. With statistics for mental health issues in the workplace worsening, one solution is to develop leaders who can create psychological safety so that people are willing to discuss previously stigmatised topics.

As the world evolves, so too does leadership style. The days of a CEO having extended boozy lunches are a distant memory; successful CEOs today are more like athletes in their self-care and commitment to personal development. Building on my deep expertise and some of the best thought leadership on authentic and purpose-driven management, I created and refined my flagship leadership-development programme to develop leaders with the mindset, skill set, behaviours and resilience necessary to deliver commercial results and evolve their firm's products and services without breaking themselves, the business, or their people in the process.

I believe that being resilient is a foundational practice to becoming a purpose-driven leader. Those who role-model resilience inspire people around them to build their resilience too. We spend a significant proportion of our lives at work; as leaders and employees we have a responsibility for creating a culture of sustainable high performance in which people can thrive and do their best work, a culture that values hitting business targets and the ability to have meaningful emotional connections with colleagues. It is my absolute conviction that happier humans are more productive, achieve more and have better self-esteem. The knock-on effect positively impacts our personal relationships and parenting too. Why stop there? When we take great care of ourselves we have more energy to give back and make a difference in our communities to create a better world.

Purpose-driven leaders

Sustainable high performance

Happier humans

Better world

FIG. 0.1: MY PURPOSE IN A NUTSHELL

Developing our personal resilience is a core life skill and the foundation on which everything else is possible. I believe we are all more capable than we realise. I encourage people to move into their 'stretch zone' so they can achieve their full potential. I consider it my duty of care to make sure they also have the resilience habits they need to support that ambition.

This is the book I wish I'd had when I joined consulting, and it's the reference book I'll keep on my desk as I continue to work towards my goals. I hope that by sharing my story and tried-and-tested resilience habits, you will commit to small consistent habits that will improve the quality of life for you, your loved ones, your business and society.

PART ONE

RESILIENCE FUNDAMENTALS

Stress is a Choice

In workshops, I consistently get a strong reaction from about one-third of the delegates when I share the belief that 'stress is a choice'. I get it, I had an uncharacteristically strong reaction the first time I heard it too. Maybe you already believe that stress is a choice – but a reminder never hurts.

CASE STUDY: MY BURNOUT – STRESS IS A CHOICE

Let me tell you about when I first heard about the belief. The doctor had signed me off work with stress and anxiety for two weeks and then another two weeks, and I was now in the waiting room of an occupational health provider close to my home. Despite almost four weeks off work and having slept for ten to twelve hours a day, every day, I was still absolutely exhausted. I was barely a shadow of my former self. I had numbed myself to life for a long time, a subconscious self-preservation strategy for getting through the day. I had booked a lunchtime appointment because I knew it would take me all morning to get showered, get dressed and eat something (the three bullets on the sticky note on the bathroom mirror). I was also only half convinced that I'd make it to the appointment, as I had become more and more reluctant to leave the house.

I went into the oak-panelled office, sat down opposite John and briefly explained the work pressures that had led to me being in his office. He asked questions. I answered. Working sixty to eighty hours a week for the last six months, working away from home, partner and step-sons, planning a wedding, converting a barn in

France every other weekend. I thought I had work-life balance, John thought I had double stress.

Question: how did I look after myself with all these pressures; did I take a lunch break? Answer: yes, three times a week. But I had rushed out, grabbed the first sandwich I saw and answered emails on my phone while I was in the queue – that didn't count as a lunch break, apparently. The interview went on.

In my jaded state I figured that John was on the side of the employer and just had to tick a few boxes to confirm I could take a longer period off work as my doctor had suggested. I was broken. I was resigned to following a medical pathway if it meant I didn't have to go back to the office. I couldn't have done, even if I had wanted to. I didn't want to. I just wanted to be under a duvet and shut the world out. As I answered more questions, I could see that John was surprised that I hadn't been in his office sooner. That wasn't much comfort – I didn't want to be there at all. Then he dropped the bombshell.

'You know... stress is a choice.'

For a moment I looked at him blankly. Had I misheard him? Was he serious?

'I'm sorry, can you repeat that?'

'Yes, of course. Stress is a choice.'

He was dead serious and looking at me with kind eyes.

> **EMPOWERING BELIEF**
> Stress is a choice.

I blinked. I waited a brief moment as the touchpaper he had just lit in my brain smouldered. And somewhere from the depths of my exhausted body came a rage I had never known. I let him have it. A verbal tirade that was accompanied by pacing up and down in front of his desk, raising my voice, pointing my finger and saying that he clearly hadn't listened to a word I had said. I was shouting out all the things I had said at work that hadn't felt heard. 'How can you possibly say that? You have no idea how it is in the real world, the pressures I'm under, the hours we are expected to work, the ludicrous demands that come in at 7.30pm for delivery to the senior stakeholders at 9am the next day, the various goalposts that are constantly changing, dealing with drama queens day and night...' I went on for about five minutes, barely drawing breath, until I had expelled six months' worth of frustration and anger. I stopped, and he was still sitting there, calm as you like, saying nothing.

I looked at him. 'Well?'

His reply probably isn't in the textbook for occupational health responses, but it was the culmination of years of experience.

'Until you're open to the idea that stress is a choice, there's nothing I can do to help you. But when you're ready, come back and we can get you back on your feet again.'

I was incandescent! I slammed the door as I left, stormed through reception and stormed home.

I sat and cried for a long time. I needed help, I was exhausted, and it seemed like the one person assigned to support me had no comprehension of what it was like to work in the real world. Great.

A few days passed, and the statement rattled around in my brain: stress is a choice. I said it out loud a few times. It didn't make sense. I looked at myself in the mirror and said it again. Yeah, because I'd choose to look like this – bloody idiot, what did he know? I did my level best to resist, but he had planted an earworm, like an annoying top ten hit that you don't like but can't get out of your head. 'Stress is a choice.'

I made another appointment. I took a carrot cake and said I had eaten all the humble pie.

John's provocation had opened up the possibility that if stress was indeed a choice then I could make a different choice. While I still didn't understand the statement, there was a deep part of me that recognised some truth in it and knew that it was my way out of the hole I was in. I clearly wasn't the first person to have burned out. Other people had been here before and got better. I chose to hear him out and see what solutions he had. John had shared a belief that started me on a path that changed everything about how I show up in the world, and I am deeply grateful for it.

I was a long way down the slippery slope to burnout before I took action. At first I didn't even realise I was stressed because everyone was, so 'stressed' felt 'normal'. Later I was working hard to look the part, knowing I was falling apart. The physical and emotional toll of burnout was enormous, and the consequences for my personal life were far-reaching.

EMPOWERING BELIEF
Taking action is a choice.

If you are already self-medicating with coffee-to-wake-up and alcohol-to-sleep, or you want to stop feeling so exhausted, please act now. If you start proactively building your resilience when you notice the early warning signs, it's much easier to get back on track, and leaving it until later might just be too late. A list of symptoms on the road to burnout is given in Appendix B.

– Angela Armstrong, strategic leadership partner

You might have to sit with this idea for a bit before it lands. That's OK. If the belief that 'stress is a choice' is new to you, please don't beat yourself up. We are all doing the best we can with the resources available to us at the time.

The following statements neatly encapsulate the broader context for the two beliefs and helped me to understand practically how I could use them to get out of the hole I was in:

The *trigger* of the stress might be outside your control; how you *perceive* the stress and how you *respond* to it are within your control.

Why you sometimes feel hijacked by stress hormones

Sometimes the trigger is outside your control; it happens 'to you'. If that trigger currently initiates a stress response from you, it can feel as though the stress is not in your control and therefore stress is not a choice.

Your beliefs about the trigger are important because when you believe that you are stressed, your body initiates a biological survival response. Your sympathetic nervous system releases cortisol and adrenalin to prepare the body for a 'flight, fight or freeze' response. The stress hormones produce well-orchestrated physiological changes that can make our heart pound, our breath quicken and our muscles tense to make us temporarily faster and stronger, so we can survive. That physical response is really helpful if you need to outrun, fight or play dead when faced with a predator, but it's less useful in day-to-day life.

INCONVENIENT TRUTH
What you think generates a chemical response in your body.

After the threat has passed, your body initiates the 'rest and digest' cycle: it eliminates the stress hormones and reactivates your digestive system and your immune system. Unfortunately, it takes your body significantly longer to eliminate the hormones than it does to create them, so many people have a backlog and find it hard to relax. If the backlog persists then the stress becomes chronic, that is, the feedback mechanism that 'turns off' the stress response stops working, and your stress hormones remain high, with serious consequences. Physical exercise can accelerate the elimination of stress hormones, and it's a necessity for anyone with a demanding role. As demands increase, pay even more attention to your physical exercise.

The long-term effects of stress on your body

The biological 'rest and digest' system is designed to repair and renew our bodies, so downtime is especially important during times of higher pressure. Chronic low-level stress is much like a motor that is idling too high for too long. Eventually, it can lead to serious health problems.

The effect of long-term chronic stress is significantly impaired physical and psychological health. Chronic stress physically modifies the neural networks in your brain in a similar way to those who suffer depression and anxiety, and can expand to other functionally connected areas, potentially causing cognitive, emotional and behavioural dysfunctions and increased vulnerability to psychiatric disorders. Dementia, and more specifically Alzheimer's disease, is a progressive neurocognitive disease. A study (Barnes et al., 2012) of more than thirteen thousand patients who were tracked over the course of fifty years found that depressive symptoms in midlife and in late life are associated with a three-fold increase in risk of developing dementia. The effect of our neurology on immunity can lead to diseases whose development has been linked to both stress and inflammation: for example, cardiovascular dysfunctions, diabetes, cancer and autoimmune syndromes (Mariotti, 2015). More preliminary research suggests that chronic social stress, often arising from poor interpersonal relationships, job or unemployment stress, poor self-esteem, and low socioeconomic status has been associated with obesity and its associated illnesses (Scott et al, 2012). Chronic stress may also contribute to obesity, both through direct mechanisms (causing people to eat more) or indirectly (decreasing sleep and exercise).

How to avoid being hijacked by stress hormones

Our emotions are triggered from two areas in our brain. The amygdala is the primitive part of our brain and the trigger point of emotion. If our life is in danger, this part retains control as part of the 'flight, fight or freeze' response. The prefrontal cortex (the 'thinking' part of our brain) is used for reasoning, inhibition and decision-making. It assesses the signals given by the amygdala. If it reasons that it is in fact our ego that is threatened and not our survival, our prefrontal cortex can inhibit the amygdala's signals, and therefore reduce the hormonal response to something more proportionate. If instead we focus on the possible survival threat (real or imagined – think of horror films) then we re-engage the amygdala and it goes on priming our system with stress hormones.

There are many ways to call on our prefrontal cortex to get involved: the classic strategy of counting to ten after feeling emotionally triggered gives our thinking brain a chance to moderate the emotion. The habits in chapter five, 'Emotions', provide other ways to identify and manage your emotions.

Four common ways that we continue the stress response unnecessarily

1. We subscribe to the banter and wear stress as a badge of honour

   Your conversations are contagious and so are the moods associated with them. Talking about stress literally causes more stress (see habit 16, 'avoid vicious cycles'). Instead, swap conversations about competing for who has the most stress with conversations about what you're doing to build your resilience habits or asking for support. Direct conversations towards solutions, not problems and wear resilience as a badge of honour. Please search 'TEDx talk how to solve the stress epidemic' and share the link to encourage more people to discuss resilience, not stress, in the workplace. We can all change the culture, one conversation at a time. Working hard does not provide a competitive advantage when everyone else is also working hard, having vitality does.

> **INCONVENIENT TRUTH**
> Your conversations are contagious.

2. We lose perspective and worrying does more harm than the threat

   The possibility of being made redundant is a concern but being made redundant won't kill you – worrying about it excessively might.

3. We mistake a threat to our ego as a threat to our survival and over-react

   I didn't realise until later that much of the rage I had directed at John in the occupational health office was a fight to maintain my identity as someone who delivered, who was on top of her game and who made informed decisions. I thought that if stress was a choice then I could not have been making good decisions, and that did not fit with my sense of self.

4. We prolong a genuine stress response long after the trigger event has passed

Consider this scenario: you're driving along the motorway, and someone overtakes you and then cuts back in front of you far too close, almost clipping your bumper. You're not alone in your car. The driver of the car in front just created a potential accident, but there was no accident. Some people would get road rage, shout energetic and colourful language at the driver in front, flash their lights and even follow them for the next half mile right on their bumper. Another driver might sharply inhale as the moment happened but quickly give the other driver space, ensure everyone in the car is OK, dismiss the other driver as reckless and get back to the conversation they were having before the near miss happened. The fact that two different people can respond to the same trigger in different ways means that the stress response is *not* biologically hard-wired for more than a microsecond. We can train ourselves to be more alert to the times when we stay 'revved up' for longer than necessary, and so experience less stress.

Once you know that stress is a choice, that taking action is a choice, and that you can moderate your emotional response to events, it feels so damn good to start regaining control that you won't give it up just to indulge in a little 'blame and complain'. The price of a stress-free life is taking radical accountability for your own well-being. You don't need permission from others to invest in your self-care. What could you do to rest and renew in some guilt-free downtime? Are you making the most of any well-being policies that your employer offers?

Soon you'll start to notice others who are firmly in the driving seat of their lives, regardless of where they are on their resilience journey from novice to mastery, and you'll know you've found your tribe.

Welcome to The Resilience Club.

How to Balance Pressure, Performance and Renewal

Pressure

We can describe the level of pressure we are feeling, or anticipate, using the terms 'comfort zone', 'stretch zone' and 'panic zone'.

When we are in our comfort zone, we are familiar with most of what we are doing, the skills and knowledge we are using, and the people we are interacting with. We're comfortable that, barring any major change of events, we will succeed at what we have set out to do. We have relaxed attention and so maintain a broad awareness and are flexible in how we approach problems.

In our panic zone we are so far outside our normal operating parameters (location, people, skill set, knowledge, experience or some other factor) that we are frightened and overwhelmed. Our survival instincts kick in: hormones circulate, and we become focused on a narrow scope for our survival.

Between the two extremes is our stretch zone, where we are challenged but the goal is only just beyond reach. For example, doing something new or something that has a degree of ambiguity or complexity. We have a reasonable expectation that if we apply ourselves diligently and get some support at the right time then we will succeed. As we become more familiar in the new situation, what was once stretch zone becomes comfort zone.

Sometimes we experience heightened pressure at work and at home at the same time, and we have to prioritise to keep the total pressure from going into panic zone. See habit 24: 'bite off what you can chew'.

A situation that one person considers to be stretch zone might be considered comfort zone or panic zone by someone else. You are the best judge of how much pressure feels right for you in each moment. Your comfort zone will change over time as you gain more experience and work on developing your resilience.

Performance

The following graph, based on a paper by Williams and Cooper (1998), shows the relationship between performance and pressure.

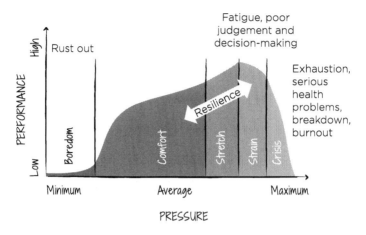

FIG. 0.2: PERFORMANCE PRESSURE GRAPH

When we are under-challenged, and not using our talents fully, our performance often suffers – we're bored. It may seem counter-intuitive, but boredom can be a source of stress for some high performers. When we are operating in our comfort zones, our performance has a wide range – from 'underperforming' to 'meets expectations', using HR terminology. It is down to the individual to self-motivate. As pressure increases, we move into our stretch zone and our performance increases as we rise to the challenge and deliver a higher level of focus, discipline and creativity. In stretch, we become more resourceful and often commit more hours to the task. Achieving a performance evaluation of 'exceeds expectations' often requires us to go above and beyond our comfort zone, ie to deliver a strong performance while in our stretch zone for an extended period.

If pressure continues to increase and we enter our panic zone, or if we have to operate in our stretch zone for longer than our personal resources allow, we move into 'strain'. As we tire, our performance starts to drop. When the pressure is relentless (as it often is in companies with a work-hard-play-hard culture) and we have exhausted our personal reserves without enough respite, we enter 'crisis'. Our performance decreases rapidly, and we experience health problems and burnout. Once you've burned out (ie had a mental and physical collapse), it is a challenge to do even the simplest tasks, and the path back to full health requires a period of extended illness absence.

> **INCONVENIENT TRUTH**
> Burnout can happen to you.

Having a toolkit of resilience practices can support us in delivering stretch performance for longer periods without detriment to our health. For example, by being able to control our emotional response to adverse events.

Renewal

Your body is an extraordinarily complex and inherently intelligent eco-system that is working constantly towards your survival, sometimes despite your best efforts to break it down and sometimes with your full support. Your body knows what it needs and gives you feedback so that you take supportive action; for example, you start to feel tired when your body needs to do some renew and repair work, so you go to sleep. When you sleep, your body renews and repairs physically (deep sleep) and processes your emotions and memory (rapid eye movement, or REM sleep). The recommendation is for seven to nine hours sleep per night for working-age adults.

> **INCONVENIENT TRUTH**
> Your body is the only place you have to live. It knows what it needs.

I mention sleep here as it's the area of self-care that many high performers skimp on even if they have good practices for renewing their energy in terms of nutrition, hydration and movement.

Listen to your body

If you do not act on the feedback your body is giving you it escalates the alert so that you take supportive action. For example, if your body is dehydrated, your body's feedback loop makes you feel thirsty, and you can decide to act on that feedback and drink fluids or eat water-rich foods like melon and cucumber. If you don't take action, the increased dehydration causes a headache. The feedback symptoms become progressively inconvenient or painful (migraine), until you take action. Ideally, that action is to resolve the root cause (dehydration) rather than to mask the symptoms or seek pharmaceutical remedies. For example, drinking caffeine for temporary alertness, or taking headache pills regularly rather than drinking 1.5 litres per day because you 'don't have time to go to the toilet'.

CASE STUDY: YOUR BODY IS WIRED FOR SURVIVAL

When I burned out, I had been wilfully ignoring the warning signs from my body for many months, and eventually I had found it easier to simply stop noticing what my body was telling me, to save me the effort of deliberately over-riding what I knew I 'should' be doing to take care of myself.

Eventually, my body did what it needed to in order to survive, and took my brain out of commission so I had no choice but to stop and rest. Burnout is a mental and physical breakdown. Once was enough to learn the lesson.

— Angela Armstrong, strategic leadership partner

EXERCISE: LISTEN TO YOUR BODY

- Take a few minutes of quiet time alone to slow down.
- Breathe deeply, relax and do a scan of your body from your toes to the top of your head focusing on how each part feels and what it needs.
- Got an itch? Scratch it. Hungry? Make time for breakfast. Shoulders tight? Do some light stretching. Taking small proactive corrective actions helps to keep your body on top form, with minimal effort, so you can enjoy the energy and mental capacity to do all the things you want to in life.
- What would be the best time for you to do your 'body scan' on a regular basis?

- A small list of symptoms ranging from exhaustion to burnout are given in Appendix B. What are your early warning signs, even before you get to 'sick and tired', that could prompt you to corrective action?

Take action

We know that we need to take action to support our natural eco-system, cleaning our teeth twice a day is common sense and common practice. We're barely even conscious of this small daily action, yet done consistently over time, it has a cumulative positive impact on our dental health. Like cleaning your teeth, using resilience habits as small daily practices, has a long-term impact.

> **EMPOWERING BELIEF**
> Because I'm worth it (do something each day your future self will thank you for).

Often common sense is not common practice. Nature has its own pace. Just as a farmer cannot yield a crop by trying to cram a full plough-seed-grow-harvest cycle into two weeks, you cannot repair your body to optimum health if you try and cram a year's worth of rest into a two-week holiday. Ideally, rest and renew daily (for example, take a lunch break) and use all your holiday entitlement (spaced throughout the year). If you fail to renew frequently or for long enough, your energy reserves deplete with potentially life-threatening consequences.

> **INCONVENIENT TRUTH**
> Your body is a natural eco-system
> and has its own pace.

As an employee, it is your responsibility to stay healthy, so you can be fully present and engaged in your work and earn your pay in exchange for your time and talents. Anything else is theft. It's harsh but true. Employers have responsibilities too. For example, fair contracts, training, and sensible work schedules appropriate to role and job description. Employer responsibilities are outside the scope of this book.

If you always have a little energy in reserve, you'll have more resources to draw on when the need arises. Specifically, to support others (if you're not in a good position yourself, you are in no position to help anyone else), to bear adversity (events such as a bereavement, accident or redundancy are statistically predictable, but you cannot plan for them), or take advantage of a great opportunity.

> **INCONVENIENT TRUTH**
> Adversity happens when you least expect it.

As you build your resilience habits it is possible that you will want to take on bigger challenges, which will require more energy. To fuel bigger ambitions, ensure that you continue to improve your physical health (sleep, nutrition, hydration and movement).

CASE STUDY: A HOLISTIC APPROACH TO RESILIENCE PREVENTS BURNOUT

Everyone has their breaking point and I definitely got close to mine. Throughout my 20s I layered on more and more demands. Exercise, family and career combined with unhealthy self-defeating beliefs took me to the edge of burnout.

In my 30s I realised things had to change when I got into a routine of frequently leaving home before 5am, cycling 250 miles per week and staying up through the night trying to be the best dad I could be. Instead of using the support networks around me, I turned inwards and tried to solve everything in my own strength.

If it wasn't for meeting Angela, and using the resilience interventions contained within this book, I am certain that I would have ended up in complete burnout. In particular, learning to manage my boundaries, do energy accounting, and express my true spirit enabled me to have guilt-free downtime, be fully present with my family and deliver my commitments at work.

– James Bulleid, Director of Technology

Sustainable High Performance

Businesses, and highly fulfilled lives, are built on your capacity to consistently deliver 'better than expected' results, year-on-year, by knowing your unique performance blueprint and resilience habits. Sustainable high performance might include an occasional short burst of peak performance.

Ideally, the demands on us are phased so that pressure peaks and tails off, then peaks and tails off again. That gives us the chance to move between our stretch and comfort zones, so we can renew and top up our resilience reserves during relatively quieter periods. Often this happens because of typical business cycles which tend to have quieter periods followed by short high-pressure periods at month end or year end. On projects, despite best planning efforts, there is usually a short pressure peak for major milestones.

Sustainable performance increase

For our career development, we can consistently increase our ability to perform at higher levels over time by operating in our stretch zone for periods that allow us to achieve a degree of proficiency, ie what was once stretch becomes comfort zone. By doing this repeatedly, we can achieve what was previously in our panic zone in approximately three steps. The lesson is to set goals that are squarely in your stretch zone, and when 'stretch' starts becoming comfortable, *and* you've had a chance to renew, then set a new stretch goal. An excellent book on applying this approach to leadership development is *Crucibles of Leadership* (Thomas, 2008). Stretch zone activities give you opportunities to learn both about leadership and how you learn.

Unfortunately, many promising careers are cut crushingly short because the increase in pressure is too fast, resulting in issues for both performance and well-being. High performance requires both high support and high challenge.

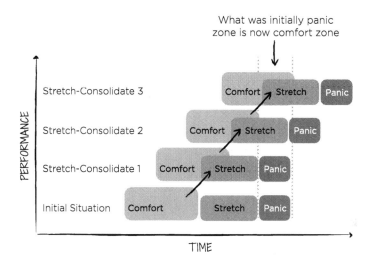

FIG. 0.3: SUSTAINABLE PERFORMANCE INCREASE

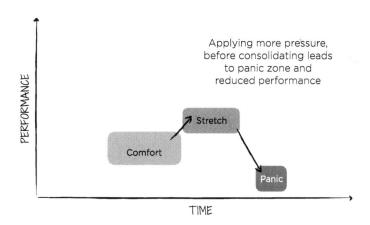

FIG. 0.4: UNSUSTAINABLE PRESSURE INCREASE

Are you tempted to make heroic efforts to deliver a 'panic zone' target? There's a *chance* you might pull it off, but you'll certainly land in an exhausted heap and need an extended period of rest and renewal before you can set off again. Sometimes the collapse comes before the achievement; either way, it's a fool's game and it's unsustainable. Sure, you *might* win the moment, but it's the ones who adopt an approach of sustainable performance increase that succeed in their career.

Reality Checks

Reality check #1 – You are not irreplaceable at work or at home

The harsh truth is that while you may be much valued, you are not irreplaceable – at work or at home. Sometimes we have to put our ego aside for a moment to see it. If the proverbial bus came along, your employer would find a good enough solution quickly and a permanent solution within months. Many families are doing a great job with a single parent or with step-parents. In the worst-case scenario, friends, family or the state would step in to fulfil your role. The reality is that if you're not available to fulfil that role fully, someone else will, or the outcome will be achieved in a different way.

> **INCONVENIENT TRUTH**
> You are not irreplaceable at work or at home.

Reality check #2 – Workplace stress has reached epidemic proportions

I burned out in 2010 when the workplace was different. Many employers are now much more aware of the impact of resilience on productivity and well-being and have updated their policies. Some employers have always supported employee well-being, because it's the human-centric thing to do. A few high-profile CEO burnout stories (such as Antonio Horta-Osorio, CEO of Lloyds Banking Group) and national campaigns such as *Time to Talk* have helped reduce the stigma of talking about mental health in the workplace. These efforts are important and should be embraced. However, the statistics on workplace stress, which have been largely unchanged since 2001, have shown signs of worsening in recent years (UK Health and Safety Executive, HSE). The HSE define work-related stress, depression or anxiety as a harmful reaction people have to undue pressures and demands placed on them at work. Workplace stress has reached epidemic proportions.

- In Great Britain in 2017/18 an estimated 15.4 million working days were lost due to work-related stress, depression or anxiety (Labour Force Survey), a prevalence rate of 1,800 per 100,000 workers. That's the equivalent of sixty-one thousand people taking one year off work.

- The numbers are under-reported: stress has forced 20% of workers to call in sick, yet the vast majority of these (93%) say they have lied to their boss about the real reason for not turning up (MIND, 2010).

- Mental health issues (stress, depression, anxiety) cost UK £10.6 billion in sickness absence in 2017 (Source MHFA).
- Presenteeism refers to people who are unwell but come into work regardless, effects include de-motivation and a decrease in productivity. The cost of presenteeism is double the cost of absenteeism (Source BUPA, 2017).
- Financial services and professional services had the highest private sector cost per employee due to mental ill-health of the seven industries reviewed (Source Deloitte Mental Health Review).

The business environment is increasingly volatile, uncertain, complex and ambiguous. Employers will play their part (which is outside the scope for this book) and on that, there is still much work to do. As individuals, we must also take responsibility for our part – you can fundamentally change your experience of the same workplace by using these resilience habits.

Reality check #3 – Health before wealth

No matter how wealthy you are, you cannot buy more time or more health.

Reality check #4 – There is no quick fix

First, the bad news: there is no quick fix, pill or intervention that can inoculate you from pressure and enable you to achieve sustainable high performance with no effort on your part. The good news: it is simpler and takes less effort than you think to significantly increase your resilience. Select a habit and practice it using the principles in habit 28, 'develop a growth mindset'.

PART TWO

THE RESILIENCE HABITS

CHAPTER ONE

The FREEDOM Model

The FREEDOM model of resilience includes habits that help you invest in your well-being as a whole person: mind, body, spirit and emotions. Imagine that you are battery-operated, and to be fully functioning you need a balance of energy in your batteries. Here are some examples of how your physical, mental, emotional and spiritual energy levels would look if your batteries were fully charged:

Physical: You regularly have more energy than you can use. You wake moments before your alarm goes off and jump out of bed energised to start the day.

Mental: You feel clear-headed, analytical or creative, decisive, able to plan, and able to switch easily between detail and strategy as the need arises. Your memory is reliable, and you enjoy embracing new problems and solving them.

Emotional: You feel grounded, able to experience a full range of emotions without feeling hijacked by them, able to connect deeply with yourself, and able to empathise with others.

Spiritual: You enjoy a sense of who you are and what makes you tick. You feel like 'you', regularly doing things that bring you joy and fulfilment and that put you in flow – where you lose all track of time. You experience a sense of oneness with nature, the universe and everything, as though everything is somehow connected.

Learning life's lessons, without the adversity

We can learn about resilience the hard way or the easy way. Most of us have developed some personal resilience the hard way – through the experience of adversity. Life can be a tough tutor: it gives you the experience first and the lesson later. Based on our life experience, we tend to have just a handful of coping strategies and rely on them for a wide variety of stress triggers. What existing coping strategies do you already have? I expect you have at least a few that promote long-term health and sanity. If you have any that might be considered sticking plasters, ignoring or numbing the issues, then look to swap them for more productive habits as you read.

The easy way to learn is from the misfortunes of others. On my road back from burnout, I researched, distilled, synthesised and simplified academic research on the survivors of traumatic events, leadership books and personal development books into a subset of practical habits. It turns out there are seven consistent categories of habits common to people who, after the initial adversity, emerged stronger and wiser. It can be helpful to have a mnemonic to retain information, so the first letter of the heading for each category spells the word FREEDOM: focus, role models, energy, emotion, downtime, optimism and meaning.

I'm also a realist: for me, research must deliver insights we can use in real life. All the habits have been tried and tested by my clients to ensure that they are relevant, practical and effective. The habits are entirely within your control, simple to understand, quick to do, can be done anywhere, cost no money and require no kit. Distilling a vast amount of information into simple and practical habits also presents a challenge, as many of the ideas may seem like common sense. You may think 'I know that', but I encourage you to ask yourself 'but do I do that?' Lasting change happens when you put what you read into action.

You are naturally creative, resourceful and *whole*; you are not two half-beings that separately inhabit your work and life existence, yet many people act as if that's true. The artificial separation itself causes strain if you deny some parts of your character. Much better to bring our whole selves to everything we do so that we can feel more congruent as individuals and are able to bring our fullest energies and resources to all situations. More on this in habit 21, 'express your true spirit'.

Before you read about the habits in detail, it may help to assess which ones you are already strong in, and which you need to develop to become more resilient.

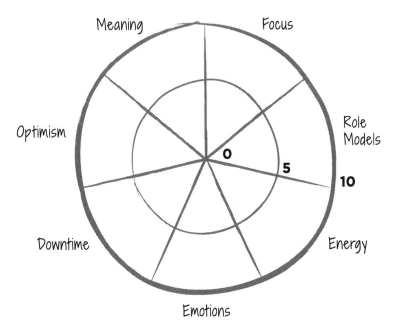

FIG. 1.1: WHEEL OF RESILIENCE

EXERCISE: ASSESSING YOUR RESILIENCE HABITS

1. Read the statements below for the categories shown on the wheel of resilience.

    Focus – I actively manage my workload demands. I direct my full attention to the one thing, within my control, that will move me forward fastest and helps avoid overwhelm.

    Role models – I have role models and a high-quality network of people who inspire me to be my best. My actions and behaviours reflect my deeply held values. I am a resilient leader who inspires others.

    Energy – I actively create, conserve and direct my energy. I am usually healthy. My energy levels allow me to deliver maximum value and influence others.

    Emotion – I have good emotional self-control. I have learned to let go of hurt and lean in to vulnerability. I can surf the emotional change curve like a pro.

    Downtime – I regularly experience joy. I can calm my mind, rest and play. I do something each week that feels true to my spirit. I create and enjoy magic moments in life.

    Optimism – I believe that 'whatever happens, I will be alright'. I take steps to build confidence in my resourcefulness, bite off what I can chew, and make choices about how I want my life to be.

    Meaning – I know why I do what I do and that enables me to dig deep in times of hardship or adversity. I ensure my self-talk is mostly positive. I learn from failure, and seek to have an impact beyond myself.

2. Complete the wheel of resilience

Score each category out of 10, where 0 means you strongly disagree with the statement and 10 means you strongly agree with the statement.

Shade each sector to reflect your score.

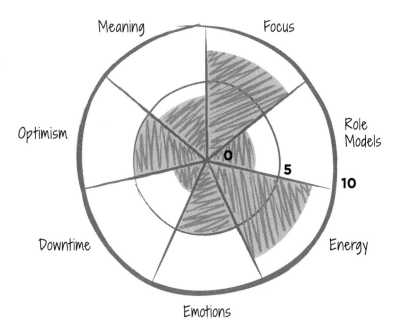

FIG: 1.2: WHEEL OF RESILIENCE (EXAMPLE)

Review – how 'lumpy' is your wheel? The idea is to develop a balance of resilience habits across the seven categories – not mastery in each individual category. That way you'll have a broad range of coping strategies to handle a variety of challenges and opportunities that arise.

3. Now you have an idea of which categories of resilience you already have strategies for and where you can extend your toolkit. Refer to the relevant chapter, scan the habits and select one that resonates. Start now with whatever you have, wherever you are: small and consistent actions make a difference.

If in doubt start here

- Create your happy file (habit 23)
- Prioritise your sphere of control (habit 1)
- Manage your boundaries (habit 13)
- Speak your truth (habit 26)

CHAPTER TWO

Focus

Sometimes the number and diversity of demands on us can feel overwhelming. Habits for gaining focus help us to consider the demands through a sequence of filters until we know the few things that will have the biggest impact. This chapter refers to focus in the sense of discipline and staying on task until something is finished. The emotional implications of where we put our focus are covered in habit 16, 'avoid vicious cycles'.

At any given moment our brains are processing thousands of pieces of information, sights, sounds and sensations which help us to make sense of the world around us. To avoid overwhelm we make choices (consciously and unconsciously) about where we put our focus and therefore what we think about most often. The part of the brain known as the rectilinear activating system is how you filter out the extraneous stimuli (circa 99%) in your environment to allow you to pay attention to what is more important or relevant to you. It's why you are still able to hear your name in a crowded place and why having bought a new car, you start to notice many more of the same make and model car on the motorway. They were always there, it's just that your focus has shifted to noticing them. What you focus on seems to expand as you start noticing events, pictures and information that are connected to our original area of focus. You can choose to focus on the past, present or future. You can choose to focus on how much you have achieved, or everything you still have to do. You can choose to focus on problems or solutions, stress or resilience – you get the idea. Focus on what you do want, not what you don't want, because the brain doesn't process negatives. For example, don't think of a pink elephant. What did you think of? A pink elephant! Instead of thinking 'I don't want to fail', think 'what must I do to succeed?' This shifts your focus to noticing opportunities and activities that can help you to succeed.

Focus is particularly important if you are supporting someone who has had a period of time off work for stress and they are doing a phased return to work. After a period of burnout, it takes a while for our thinking to become fully sharp again, and ambiguity can quickly create overwhelm. Support people by being specific about what needs to be done, offering some suggestions on how to do it, and being available in the background if they have questions.

When it comes to applying deliberate conscious effort, there is no such thing as multitasking; trying to do more than one thing at a time divides our focus and increases the mental effort of switching between tasks. Having focus is about directing your full attention to the one thing that will move you forward fastest and staying with it until it is done. Focus until it's finished.

Focused repetition also helps with the learning process. When first learning new skills or knowledge, we are consciously incompetent. As we learn how to do the task, we have to practice and apply ourselves to it; this is the conscious competence stage. With additional focused repetition, the neural pathway for that information becomes stronger and we develop unconscious competence so that we can perform the skill so easily it seems unconscious. Consider how much effort it took you to learn to drive a car compared to the effort of driving today. If we learn something but don't put it into practice, the knowledge quickly dissipates. Small consistent actions that become daily habits build your resilience more effectively than heroic efforts once in a while.

Why it matters

Gaining focus on a few high-impact actions helps to reduce overwhelm and direct our efforts productively towards our highest priorities. Focused repetition enables us to maximise the return on investment in training so that the new ways of working become second nature. Being aware that what we focus on alerts us to watch out for confirmation bias during recruitment and selection activities and deliberately seek diversity.

CASE STUDY: FOCUS ON THREE PRIORITIES TO DIRECT PRODUCTIVE EFFORT

I have career-driven ambitions and high personal standards. I have found that focusing your attention is a key factor to achieving stretch outcomes. Most recently, I accepted a position at a fast-paced automotive company where I am managing the turnaround of an underperforming project. I need to simultaneously solve historical technical issues, deliver present milestones and plan future deliverables. By directing my focus towards the issues that have the largest impact, ie legal, quality and cost, I am able to prioritise the deliverables. Taking this approach has clarified my thinking, and grown my confidence, resulting in the approval of several option papers that demonstrated to stakeholders the root cause of problems and proposed solutions. Solutions I then delivered successfully with my team.

– Akram Habib, Lead Project Engineer

This chapter includes the following habits:

1. Prioritise your sphere of control – direct your energy and effort towards those areas that are within your control, so you use your energy productively.

2. Direct your focus – decide on a few vital outcomes that are important and develop the discipline to deliver on your commitments.

3. Solve the root cause of the problem – taking time to investigate a situation more fully can prevent fire-fighting and resolve multiple issues at once.

4. Make a decision – decision-making frameworks to avoid overwhelm and analysis paralysis, so you have longer to act on the decision made.

5. Simplify to one piece of paper – reducing the cognitive load for yourself and others and providing clarity on your highest priority outcomes.

Habit 1: Prioritise Your Sphere of Control

By focusing the majority of your effort on what is within your control, you can reduce stress and release time and energy for the things you can control. One of the fastest ways to reduce your stress is the oldest habit in the book, based on the original 'locus of control' (Rotter, 1966). Prioritise those things that are directly in your sphere of control: your beliefs, your thoughts and your actions in this present moment. Everything else is outside your control (for example, the weather) and time spent trying to change it or wishing it were different is simply a waste of energy. To alleviate stress: let go, mentally and emotionally, of those things that are outside your control. As leaders, we want to influence other people's mindset; for example, by giving our support or opinions. We can also influence behaviour through negotiated expectations and standards, even enforce those standards by contract or practice, but it's still not control. The other party can still exert their free will and accept the consequences. The only effective way of changing another person is by changing yourself. Show them the way.

Other people's words, thoughts, actions, body, emotions, decisions, goals. Where they live/work, how they invest their time

My example, support, collaboration, cooperation, opinion, persuasion. What I teach/share

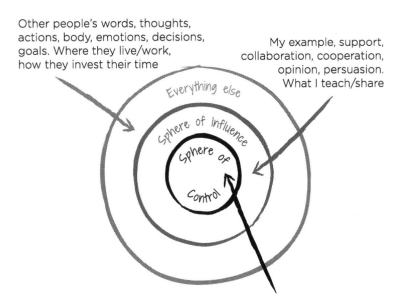

My words, thoughts, actions, body, emotions, decisions, goals. Where I live/work, how I invest my time

FIG 2.1: SPHERE OF CONTROL

TOP TIPS: KEEPING YOUR FOCUS IN YOUR SPHERE OF CONTROL

- Focus on the present or the future. You cannot change the past.
- Focus on your response. You cannot control events or people that trigger stress.
- Focus on developing yourself. You can't do the work for others.
- Be your own benchmark. There's always someone wealthier or smarter than you.
- Delegate appropriate control when you go on holiday.

EXERCISE: PRIORITISE YOUR SPHERE OF CONTROL

1. Complete the first column in the table below. List your current priorities, projects, to-do list and anything that generates a negative emotional response for you. There are lists of frequently occurring triggers of stress in Appendix A.

2. Tick one of the columns to the right to allocate each activity to the relevant sphere.

Things I currently give energy	Sphere of control	Sphere of influence	Everything else

Reflect on where the balance is between the three spheres. Is it where it needs to be?

3. Take any necessary actions:

Sphere of control: fiercely own and deliver on your commitments (say what you'll do, do what you say). If something *should* be within your control but you don't have the necessary control (time, resources, authority) then renegotiate with your line manager.

Sphere of influence: consider how you can extend your influence by being a better role model/colleague/friend/lover. Consider where your influence might be unwanted and whether it is beneficial for you/them to continue your efforts.

Everything else: Delete it from your list (if appropriate tell others you have done so) and don't give it any more time or energy. If you still feel emotionally attached see habit 14, 'accept what is'. If you regularly focus on specific things in this category, consider writing yourself a 'to-don't' list so they are easier to spot next time (eg getting frustrated by rush-hour traffic).

The habits in this book are transformational. Many high performers see abundance and want everyone to rise, so if you share these habits, remember that whether others do any personal development is outside your control! Many people will, some won't; it's their choice.

> **EMPOWERING BELIEF**
> I can't do the work for them.

Benefits for you

By prioritising action on what is within your control, you can reduce stress and release time and energy for the things you can control.

Benefits for others

Work you delegate to others is within their sphere of control, reducing their stress. Others are clearer on what you are held accountable for (control) and when you are playing a supporting (influencing) role. You are no longer meddling in tasks they own, which are outside your sphere of control!

Related habits

- Direct your focus (habit 2)
- Accept what is (habit 14)

Habit 2: Direct Your Focus

Directing your focus is the practice of identifying specific outcomes to expend your energy within your sphere of control. It's also about having the discipline to do what you planned and staying focused until the task is finished. Having lots of part-finished tasks scatters our attention and our energy and can lead to overwhelm.

Defining your outcome

Stephen R. Covey (2004), in *The 7 Habits of Highly Effective People* (a book that has sold over 25 million copies) includes 'begin with the end in mind'. That is, envision what you want in the future, so you can work and plan towards it. By developing an outcome-oriented mindset you remain open to different ways of reaching the same end and are less disheartened if the first attempt is not fruitful. I often refer to this as tight and loose: tight on the outcome, loose on the approach. For example, when delivering training, I am focused on the agreed learning outcomes for the delegates, but given a broad range of needs in the room, I have to remain flexible on pace and approach to provide the best learning experience.

EXERCISE: DEFINE YOUR OUTCOME
AROUND PERSONAL RESILIENCE

To practice defining an outcome, start with why you picked up this book:

1. Result: What do you want to be able to be, do or have once you've improved your resilience? Phrase your answers positively and come up with what you *do* want, not what you *don't* want. Perhaps you want to *be* more relaxed, or to *do* things you don't currently have the energy for or *have* a long and healthy retirement. Ideally, make this something measurable, or write a paragraph describing the future state using powerful and emotive language.

2. Purpose: When your resilience is as you'd like it to be, what is possible for you? What does it give you a sense of? For example, having a long and healthy retirement will mean you can play active games with your grandchildren... even though you are not yet a parent! It will give you a sense of longevity.

3. Action: What are the top ten actions that will make the most difference to you achieving that outcome? When will you do them? What other resources do you need?

4. Now that you have an idea of the three-step process, define three specific, measurable, achievable, relevant and time-bound outcomes you want to achieve in the next week and prioritise your time and resources to achieve them. Maintain the discipline of focusing on outcomes, not tasks. For example, the task of creating a presentation for the board is intended to create the outcome of getting buy-in for a recommended way forward.

Exercising discipline

We can waste considerable effort planning and re-planning our diaries, or by switching between tasks because we're 'not in the mood', 'it's raining', 'it's Friday', or we 'don't have the energy' to do the thing we had planned to do. Exercising discipline requires us to exercise self-management of our emotions (more on that in chapter five) and to follow through on our intentions. There's no science to it: decide what you are going to do – do it – celebrate – repeat. These simple mantras can assist you:

- Because I said I would (the title of a TEDx talk by Alex Sheen)
- Make a decision, stick to it
- Do it once, do it right
- Plan the work, work the plan
- I've started so I'll finish
- Clear desk policy, one thing at a time

'Actions speak louder than words.'
– Abraham Lincoln, President of the United States 1861–1865

Benefits for you

By directing your focus, you will set targets that help you progress and create a bias for action. When we keep the promises we make to ourselves, it improves our sense of self-efficacy and creates a results-fuelled optimism for the future.

Benefits for others

When your focus is more directed, you will stay on task (and therefore won't meddle in other people's areas of work, or with how they go about achieving an outcome). Your deliberately focused effort will yield results faster, benefiting colleagues. By keeping your commitments, others can more reliably plan their work.

Related habits

- Prioritise your sphere of control (habit 1)
- Solve the root cause of the problem (habit 3)
- Maximise value with minimal effort (habit 12)

Habit 3: Solve the Root Cause of the Problem

This habit is about taking the time to analyse an issue thoroughly before you commit resources. When the same problem happens more than once it's often because you're tackling the symptoms, not the root cause (AKA fire-fighting). For example, you'll have to put air in your tyres every week if you don't fix the slow puncture you got when you drove over a nail in the road. Or the person who always gives you a frosty reception because there's unresolved tension from a previous encounter. Ultimately, fire-fighting is a drain on your time and energy, and it can also reduce your spirit if it occurs over an extended period. Remember, even firefighters don't just put out fires; they tackle the causes by educating people about how to prevent a fire.

Five why's

Being curious and asking 'Why?' five times can take you back to the root cause. It might take longer to get to the bottom of it, and you might need to test several hypotheses, but you'll save time and energy in the long run.

EXAMPLE: ESTABLISHING THE ROOT CAUSE USING THE FIVE 'WHY'S'

Problem as first stated: I have more work to do than hours in the day, again.

Why? My workload gets added to faster than I can finish the tasks I already have.

Why? The tasks are more complex and more reliant on stakeholder contribution than anticipated, even after I apply the 80/20 rule (see habit 2, 'direct your focus').

Why? The complexity and timing of the task were not adequately thought through before I accepted it, and it is summer, so colleague availability is an issue.

Why? I'm not the only one who is overwhelmed with work. My stakeholders take a 'dump it and run' approach to 'delegation', because they are also overwhelmed.

Why? As an organisation, we have a pattern of fire-fighting rather than solving the root cause so that we fix issues once and for all.

Solution: Stop. Take a step back. Discuss with your relevant stakeholders to identify the root cause of the issues, not the symptoms, and what the actions are to resolve.

Be careful: only use the 'five why's' technique with situations, not people, or you'll quickly have them in tears by questioning their deeply held core values.

Define the problem in solvable terms

In complex situations, coming up with a key question enables us to direct our resources to the crux of the matter in the most efficient way. To break the problem down, a useful framework is 'situation, complication, key question'.

Situation	Statements of indisputable facts about the problem.
Complication	Qualitative/quantitative facts on why the status quo must change.
	Qualitative/quantitative criteria for evaluating potential solutions.
Key question	The simple one-part question which, when answered, unlocks a solution to the identified problem.
Executive sponsor	Named individuals with control of resources.
Decision-makers	Named individuals who will decide whether the proposed solution resolves the key question and is aligned to values and strategic direction.
Quality criteria	What are the features of a high-quality solution?
Scope	What is in/out of scope for consideration?

Complete the table with one of your own problems.

An example of defining the problem in solvable terms:

Situation	Workplace stress has reached epidemic proportions.
	Many employers have started to implement well-being practices.
	Business remains volatile, uncertain, complex and ambiguous.
Complication	Workplace culture is slow to change.
	Leaders are often stressed and therefore not resilient role models.
	Individuals need a solution now.
	Those in need of resilience have little time to read a whole book.
	Nomadic professionals have minimal routine and frequently work long hours or overnight away from home – no access to 'kit'.
Key question	How can I best share what I have learned about resilience in a format that recognises real-life constraints yet still delivers impact?
Executive sponsor	Angela Armstrong (funds to write, publish and publicise book).
Decision-makers	Beta readers and publishing team; readers.
Quality criteria	Practical quick reference book, professional standard, whole person approach, incorporates current research, tried-and-tested habits.
Scope	In scope – habits the individual can do that are entirely within their sphere of control.
	Out of scope – everything else.

Root causes of stress such as health, finances and relation-ships are outside the scope of this book but there are books I highly recommend in Useful Resources.

Benefits for you

By solving the root cause, your effort becomes specific to a narrow set of actions and saves on futile effort. Getting to the bottom of a situation so it does not recur is hugely satisfying and reduces unplanned disruption (fire-fighting) in future.

Benefits for others

Solving the root cause saves the ongoing effort to solve the recurring symptoms of the problem. The analysis required to determine the root cause often involves wider consulta-tion and allows others, with diverse views on how to solve the problem, to feel valued. Solving a recurring problem in a targeted way often solves related problems at the same time, which eases tension for others involved too.

Related habits

- Direct your focus (habit 2)
- Make a decision (habit 4)

Habit 4: Make a Decision

This habit is about decision frameworks that enable you to spend less time making decisions and more time acting on them. When we are finding a decision difficult to make, we can get stuck in 'analysis paralysis'. Indecision saps energy and wears us down mentally. Because we take longer to make the decision, we have less time to take action and get results. Sometimes, procrastination means that we miss the boat altogether.

To put decision-making into context, there are few decisions that cannot be undone. Usually, a 'good enough' (habit 12, 'maximise value with minimal effort') decision moves us to action and we can re-assess as time passes and further information comes to light.

> **EMPOWERING BELIEF**
> Progress, not perfect.

EXERCISE: DECISION-MAKING FRAMEWORK

Step 1: Is this a decision I am empowered to make? If no, return to sender or redirect to the appropriate person.

Step 2: Gain perspective. A year from now, will I even remember making this decision? Is it a small (daily task), medium (buying a house, changing jobs) or large decision (getting married, amputating a leg)?

Step 3: Define up to six quality criteria for a 'good enough' decision before starting the research. For example, if you're choosing a new supplier you might include ability to meet defined need, time, cost, ease of working with, and culture fit.

Step 4: Set yourself a time limit for making a 'good enough' decision.

Step 5: Decide under what circumstances (if any) you can revisit the decision. For example, if you initiate a temporary work-around solution, when will the full solution become available?

Step 6: Use the techniques below to make the decision and move on.

Technique 1: Make fewer decisions. For example, when delegating, focus on the outcome you want, rather than being prescriptive about how it should be achieved. First, decide *who* is best placed (within their sphere of control) and most cost-effective to complete the task. Explain the outcome and the means of evaluating a good solution, such as time, cost and quality (*what*). Then explain the importance of the task (*why*) and the urgency (*when*). Provide signposts to any key resources that might help. Then let the other person contribute their time and talents to decide *how, where* and *when* they are going to do the task to meet the deadline and quality standard.

Technique 2: Spend less time on small decisions. For small decisions (such as responding to an email), Apply the '4Ds' filtering questions in this order:

1. Delete: Can I delete it or ignore it?

2. Delegate: Can I delegate it?

3. Do it: Can I do it quickly and easily now?

4. Defer: Set aside time in your calendar (with others, when you have time, or when you have the information you need) to make the decision later.

Technique 3: Consider medium decisions. For medium decisions (such as promotions and investment decisions), use qualitative and quantitative data to balance decision-making and minimise bias.

Management consulting is built on 2 × 2 decision grids. By plotting options against the two most important parameters for the decision, you can understand the 'landscape' of possible solutions. One of the most recognised grids is cost-benefit for investment decisions. For promotions, you could assess candidates by plotting them against the parameters of potential (likely future performance) and performance (current performance). If a candidate has more potential than their current performance, and their current performance is 'almost' at the level of the role they would be promoted into, then it's likely they would get shortlisted for an interview panel. For prioritising work, Stephen Covey (2004) states that effort spent on urgent (time-sensitive) and important (strategically advantageous) activity, to be highly effective, should follow these percentages: not urgent and important (60%), urgent and important (25%), urgent and not important (14%), not urgent and not important (1%). A template is available, see www.TheResilienceClub.co.uk. An excellent little book called *The Decision Book* (Krogerus and Tschappeler, 2017) contains fifty models for strategic thinking for improving and understanding yourself and others.

Technique 4: Consider life decisions. For life decisions, three techniques are:

1. Make a balanced decision by considering your core values (habit 8, 'achieve personal alignment') and purpose (habit 29, 'find your purpose').

2. Use the 'fast-forward' approach: what is the likely consequence of making different decisions three, five and ten years from now?

3. If you consider these and are still wavering between decisions, flip a coin. It sounds glib, but your immediate response to the result will be from your intuition, and that's the culmination of your life lessons. That response is worth considering.

Benefits for you

Being decisive saves time and energy and allows your rational mind to be settled, which helps you switch off and relax.

Benefits for others

When others are exposed to your decision-making process, they learn about your values and priorities. Over time they can come to predict your likely response and use the same process to think things through for themselves, either agreeing and acting autonomously, or presenting relevant evidence as an alternative suggestion.

Related habits

- Solve the root cause of the problem (habit 3)
- Simplify to one piece of paper (habit 5)
- Achieve personal alignment (habit 8)
- Find your purpose (habit 29)

Habit 5: Simplify to One Piece of Paper

In a world where information is freely and readily available online, it's easy to succumb to complexity and overwhelm. There is great art and considerable value in simplification. A core skill that everyone aspiring to leadership would benefit from is the ability to write a compelling one-page executive summary. This is a visible demonstration of your ability to determine what's urgent, important or just interesting about the matter at hand. The ability to routinely lessen cognitive overload for others is a core efficiency differentiator when seeking promotion or directing your team. It takes considerable effort to distil only the key messages from an argument, and you can only do that well if you truly understand the content. Your readers will appreciate the time you have saved them. Some useful one-pagers based on the content of this book can be found at www.TheResilienceClub.co.uk

A strong executive summary includes:

Brief description of what the summary is about (key question)	
What?	Why it is important (situation) / why (complication) was the work done?
	What are the major findings/results?
So what?	What do you propose / recommend as next steps?
	Why did you choose this option?
Now what?	What is the next step?
	What do you need from the reader (resources, approval)?

A picture paints a thousand words – the speed with which infographics, mind maps, book summaries and one-page summaries go viral on social media is a testament to their usefulness. Whether your one page is for an internal or external audience, make sure it contains accurate and pertinent information. In particular, always check the source and sample size of any statistics.

TOP TIPS: SIMPLIFY

- In your personal life, take the time to create a single page for bank holiday dates, the birthdays of family and friends, renewal dates for car and house insurance, tax cycles and local school term times.
- For projects, show all the key milestones for the project on a single page.

- To organise task lists, create a focused and prioritised list on one page.

- For progress tracking, include a small number of key performance indicators to cut through the noise and inform your decision-making. For example, projects usually have a one-page status update that lists the current status of ongoing activities, project milestones completed or due, escalated risks and issues, requests for support and celebrations to share.

The act of distilling content requires effort, but you learn in the process and come to know what is important, what can be omitted. You will also hone your key messages to share with others, increasing your influence.

Benefits for you

Simplifying complex information helps you banish overwhelm and increase your focus, supporting consistency of action and communications. Distilling the most important information reduces cognitive load, saves time and reassures you that you won't forget the most important things, even when life gets busy.

Benefits for others

By simplifying information and drawing out the most important messages, you save others time and effort.

Related habits

- Direct your focus (habit 2)
- Solve the root cause of the problem (habit 3)
- Make a decision (habit 4)
- Shape your leadership identity (habit 9)

CHAPTER THREE

Role Models

A role model is someone whose beliefs, attitudes and behaviours inspire us. Role models can be living or dead, older or younger, real or fictional, someone you have met or someone you have not. You can also have anti-role models: people whose beliefs, skills, attitudes or behaviours inspire us to be the opposite.

Role models often include parents, children and wider family members, teachers, clergy, friends, coaches, peers, colleagues and sports heroes. It would be unrealistic to have a single role model who embodies all the beliefs, attitudes and behaviours you aspire to. To create our unique best, we can aspire to the best bits from different people – think of it as a role model buffet.

A resilience role model I admire is Serbian–Australian Nick Vujicic. He was born with a rare genetic disorder that means he has no arms and no legs, but he makes his living as a motivational speaker. He has a wife and two children. His tag line is 'no arms, no legs, no worries'. If ever I think I'm having a rough day, I look at one of Nick Vujicic's many short video clips on YouTube and that soon resets my perspective on the situation I'm tackling.

If you are aiming to improve your fitness or endurance, you might be inspired by local heroes or marathon runners. I was inspired by a TED talk by Diana Nyad, a woman who swam over one hundred miles from Florida to Cuba at age sixty-five, having failed at four previous attempts since her twenties. TED talks are inspiring, high-quality, eighteen-minute speeches, and there are thousands online at www .ted.com.

Why it matters

Role models are important in terms of resilience because we learn by modelling others – if we can see someone who has already achieved something that we want to achieve, we know it is possible and they can show us the way.

Role models who have experienced some of the same adversity we are currently facing can give us hope that the situation will pass and there are brighter times ahead.

Whether you intend to be one or not, you are a role model, or an anti-role model, for others who are observing your behaviour. You may as well be a good role model.

The habits in this chapter support us to deliberately decide who we allow to influence how we show up in the world:

6. Use role models and mentors – notice who already models the skills, knowledge and qualities you aspire to, so you can learn from the best.

7. Design your peer group – choose to be surrounded most often by people who lighten your mood or help you to grow as a person and as a professional.

8. Achieve personal alignment – discover what is most important to you and how it impacts your day-to-day decision-making.

9. Shape your leadership identity – taking time to define and practice who you want to be as a leader. Being authentic is the most effective and sustainable way to lead.

Habit 6: Use Role Models and Mentors

A role model is someone whose beliefs, attitudes and behaviours inspire us. A mentor is someone we have direct access to: a real person who is alive and of whom we can ask questions and receive guidance. You might be able to persuade your role model to be a mentor to inspire and support you. They could be mentoring you on a volunteer or paid basis. Often delegates on a high-potential talent programme are mentored by someone who is two promotions ahead of them in the company.

Define:

- Who already inspires you to be the best version of yourself in different areas of your life, such as health, fitness, family, relationships, finances, and hobbies?
- Which managers or leaders would you consider to be a role model in your professional network?
- Pick the best bits from several role models to create your own idea of what it would mean for you to be the best, most resilient, version of yourself.
- If no names come to mind do some research online or ask your peers. For example, Brené Brown for courage. Find a motivational video online that inspires you. Many of them tell stories of perseverance through adversity and achieving greatness.

Engage:

- If you're lucky, one of your role models might also be a mentor. Can you negotiate a mentor–mentee relationship with the people you have identified (typically a one-hour meeting every two months)? What would you like to get from that relationship, and what insight or effort could you offer in return?
- If they are not available to you personally, what can you learn from their published content? Borrow a book or attend a free taster seminar or webinar hosted by one of your role models.

Model/learn:

- Observe one of your role models. Break down the belief, skill, attitude or behaviour you want to emulate. Watch how they do it, then try it yourself.

- Ask your role model, a coach or a mentor to provide feedback on your progress towards the improvements you want to make.

- Guard against comparison fatigue; it's as easy to get disheartened as inspired at this point. Remember you are consciously raising the bar on your performance expectation – if you're not sensing a gap then you've probably played too safely with the people you have identified.

- Be the role model or mentor you wish you had. Who observes and models what you do? Who finds *you* inspiring? How can you increase your visibility to have more influence as a role model for others?

In addition to role models and mentors, you might also consult advisors, who have expertise you want access to, even if they do not inspire you in terms of how they show up in the world.

Benefits for you

By noticing the traits and success of others, you can learn from them and become more discerning of how you want to show up in the world, inspiring and informing your internal set of standards.

Benefits for others

Whether you choose to be a role model or not, others are observing your behaviours and deciding whether you are a role model, benign, or an anti-role model.

Related habits

- Design your peer group (habit 7)
- Shape your leadership identity (habit 9)
- Be kind to yourself (habit 27)
- Develop a growth mindset (habit 28)

Habit 7: Design Your Peer Group

The people who enjoy the most success (and get invited to all the must-attend parties) work hard at building their network and associate with people who inspire them to be, do, or have more. We all work hard at excelling in our chosen profession through our careers or businesses, but talent alone doesn't cut it. Your designed peer group is the five people you spend most time with, whom you can nurture one-to-one relationships over the years as you grow as a person and as a professional, and who call you forth to your highest self. Your peer group comprises people who bring something to the relationship in an area(s) of interest to you. The relationship is reciprocal in that you also add value for them; for example, by offering a sounding board on your own areas of expertise.

The idea of deliberately designing your peer group, rather than leave it to chance, is based on two main premises, six degrees of separation, and peer influence.

Six degrees of separation is the theory that everyone and everything is six or fewer steps away, by way of introduction, from any other person in the world, so that a chain of 'a friend of a friend' statements can be made to connect any two people in a maximum of six steps. When I first heard this theory, and slightly tongue-in-cheek, I challenged the person who told me to connect me with George Clooney in six degrees – it turns out a friend of a friend of a friend knows his cleaner – I was staggered! In the past twenty years the parlour game 'six degrees of Kevin Bacon' went from light amusement for some university graduates to a philanthropic organisation connecting celebrities to causes and raising millions of dollars (www.sixdegrees.org). As social media platforms continue to evolve and expand the ability to discover who knows who expands too. In 2016, Facebook calculated that 'each person in the world (at least among the 1.59 billion people active on Facebook) is connected to every other person by an average of three and a half other people' (Bhagat et al., 2016).

'You are the average of the five people you spend the most time with.'
– Jim Rohn, American entrepreneur, author and motivational speaker

The quote relates to the law of averages, which is the theory that the result of any given situation will be the average of all outcomes. Whether we like the idea or not, our experience tells us that we are greatly influenced by the relationships we have with the five people who are closest to us. We are more affected by our environment than we think. Recall that in the section called 'stress is a choice' you learned that our conversations are contagious; having peers that wear stress as a badge of honour creates more stress, having peers who discuss resilience lessens stress and normalises self-care practices that support high performance.

EXERCISE: DESIGN YOUR PEER GROUP

1. Write the names of the ten to twelve people you spend the most time with.

2. For each person, decide if they are A-list, B-list or C-list:

    a. A-list people lighten your mood and are playing the game of life at the same or a higher level than you. They are positive and supportive, but also inspire, critique and challenge you.

    b. B-list people are same-level peers – you're comfortable around each other.

    c. C-list people lower your mood or do not contribute strongly to the relationship.

3. Think about which areas are important to you, such as health, relationships or finance. You'll want a peer for each, sometimes the same person covers more than one area. Who else would you like in your A-list peer group of five people? Perhaps a mindset coach, a critical friend who will tell you the truth, someone

further ahead of you in your chosen career, a strong connector or someone who loves you unconditionally.

4. Now the big question. Looking at the people in your A-list (designed or actual), would they consider you to be in their A, B or C-list? How can you show up more powerfully as an A-list peer and make time to strengthen the relationship?

5. If your current peer group is not as you would design it, consider what action you'll take. Recognise that you always have four choices (habit 25):

Change it: some people you might not want to spend as much time with (for example, work colleagues or family) and you'll need to have some tricky conversations or change the nature of how you spend time together

Change me: work on your own resilience so you are less susceptible to negative effects and continue showing up as your best in the hope of influencing them

Accept it: the discomfort of change is not worth the upside of a designed peer group

Opt out: create a new work arrangement or spend less time on that relationship

---

It might be uncomfortable to create some distance from existing unhelpful relationships. Seeking out new relationships requires a bit of effort in terms of researching who to know and how to connect with them. Putting yourself in new situations might require you to push beyond current comfort zones.

Benefits for you

You will feel valued – you are also sharing your knowledge, skills, expertise or connections with them. You'll have a sense of safety, certainty and community. You'll make faster and more considered decisions with less effort and get connected to people who can help you. You'll also benefit in terms of personal growth and increased influence, not to mention all the fun and fulfilment from hanging out with people you admire and respect.

Benefits for others

The people in your peer group will feel as though their input is valued and they'll benefit from your contribution to the relationship. Those around you will benefit from the ripple effect of your ability to make faster and more considered decisions.

Related habits

- Direct your focus (habit 2)
- Make a decision (habit 4)
- Maximise value with minimal effort (habit 12)
- Know you always have four choices (habit 25)

Habit 8: Achieve Personal Alignment

Personal alignment helps us with our resilience because when we know who we are and what we stand for, we show up more authentically and make choices that align with what's important to us. A core value is a principle or belief that you view as being of central importance. Our core values are the guiding principles that dictate our behaviour and action. Some examples are honesty, quality, family, balance and accountability (there's a list in Appendix C). Knowing our core values helps us to prioritise where we spend our time, money and energy. When we are aware of those values, we know what we will exert ourselves to protect.

> 'If you don't stick to your values when they're being tested, they're not values; they're hobbies.'
> – Jon Stewart, American writer and entertainer

When we have clarity on our core values, we tend to notice more easily when circumstances or other people pull us away from them, and a degree of internal tension can arise. This can often happen in the workplace, and it's one reason employers recruit, and candidates select, based on workplace culture. Workplace culture is 'how things get done around here', and it includes the company values. Intentionally or otherwise, both employer and candidate are seeking to answer the question 'Does this person or company feel like a good fit?' If there is a good overlap between the organisation's values and yours, the organisation will see behaviour that's more aligned to its brand, and you will feel less internal tension.

First try this quick way to uncover your core values: think of a time when you felt proud or overjoyed: this was probably the result of something that was aligned to your core values. Examples may include feeling a sense of joy when your child learned to walk or feeling proud when your hard work was formally recognised; if so, your core values would be family and achievement. Also think of times when you had a strong negative emotional response to something: it's likely that the situation was crossing one of your core values. Examples may include feeling a sense of injustice or a betrayal of trust; if so, justice and trust are two of your core values. See if you can write down the six core values that most resonate with you. If your core values did not surface easily using these prompts, then you may find that creating your lifeline story works better for you.

EXERCISE: CREATE YOUR LIFELINE STORY

1. Consider three positive and three negative pivotal events that shaped who you are today, your character and what has meaning for you.

2. Tell someone else what these events were, what they meant to you and what you learned. Tell them about the events in the order that they happened. This is your 'lifeline'.

3. Ask your listener to do just that – listen, without asking questions – while you finish telling them your lifeline. Ask them to identify and write down any values that they hear in what you are saying as they listen (they could use the short list of values in Appendix C).

4. When you have finished explaining your lifeline, offer your listener the opportunity to ask one or two clarifying questions, and then ask them to tell you the values they wrote down.

5. Keep five or six of the values they offer or add your own until you have a set that feels like a good starting point for you. Select values that express the best of who you are.

6. Review the set after a couple of weeks to see if they still feel right. Adjust your set of values if necessary.

'Our values decide our character. Our character decides our value.'
     – James Kerr, 2013

EXERCISE: ACTING IN ACCORDANCE WITH YOUR CORE VALUES

1. For each of your six core values consider the degree to which you are expending your time, energy and money on activity relevant to that value in your daily activities. Mark the value as either 'operational' (you do it regularly) or 'aspirational' (currently intention more than action).

2. Which are your top two core values (the two that you use most, operationally)? Your top two have the most impact on how you show up day to day and how you prioritise.

3. Recognise the implications of holding those top two core values and challenge yourself to adopt a higher standard. For example, if honesty is one of your core

values, some conversations may be difficult. Do you
have them (see habit 26, 'speak your truth') or do
you avoid the topic or the person? Is withholding
information lying by omission? Is a white lie OK?
What is the standard you hold yourself to around the
core value of honesty?

CASE STUDY: COURAGE OF CONVICTIONS TO SPEAK UP

An award-winning track record earned me the
opportunity to lead on the most significant
transformation project we'd had in years. Moving from
business as usual to change management was new
territory and I was fortunate to engage Angela as my
coach. We did an exercise on discovering my core values
and it has proven invaluable when, inevitably, there are
tough calls to make in leadership. Knowing my core
values and taking the time to get personally aligned
with what needs to be said, gives me the courage of my
convictions to speak up in critical moments. The right
thing isn't always the easy thing, but leadership is about
doing the right thing.

– Ian Black, Head of Customer Service, Coventry
Building Society

Benefits for you

Knowing, and acting in accordance with, your values can
offer you a sense of internal peace and you are less likely to
feel emotionally conflicted, even if you disagree with others.

When you know your values, it takes much less effort to stand up for what you believe is right, make decisions, to take more risks and to consistently show your values through your actions.

Benefits for others

When you act in line with your values, others sense your authenticity. This increases their emotional safety and trust in you.

Related habits

- Make a decision (habit 4)
- Shape your leadership identity (habit 9)
- Know you always have four choices (habit 25)
- Find your purpose (habit 29)

Habit 9: Shape Your Leadership Identity

Your leadership identity might also be called your character strengths – it's who you are as a person. Identity is distinct from talent strengths (what you are skilled at) and core values (moral compass) although there may be some overlap. For example, if honesty is a core value then being honest is a congruent character trait.

Children are often uninhibited in how they show up in the world, and they are frequently labelled by influential adults as 'clever', 'cheeky', 'loving', 'adventurous', 'quiet' and so on. When we hear those messages consistently, we tend to live up to the label and over time it informs our identity. As adults who are seeking to become better versions of ourselves, we can define our own identity. We can choose to keep those elements of our character that we want to embrace and let go of anything that no longer feels relevant or is no longer serving us. As leaders our potential to influence is multiplied, so defining who we want to be is even more important. The ability to define our identity as adults is a gift.

'Our history is not our destiny.'
 – Alan Cohen, American businessman,
   pharmaceutical

EXERCISE: SHAPE YOUR LEADERSHIP IDENTITY

Ponder any, or all, of these questions and see what character qualities consistently emerge as being important about who you are as a leader today.

1. What existing character qualities do you prioritise in how you show up?

2. What five words would those closest to you use to describe you? Ask them!

3. What words do others use to describe you that make you feel the best version of yourself?

4. What character traits are you most passionate about role-modelling for others?

5. Which of the VIA Classification of character strengths and virtues are you drawn to (search online for a list)? Examples include, curiosity, honesty, kindness, fairness, humility and humour.

Shortlist your top five to eight character traits then find a quiet spot, set your ego and rational thinking aside. Consider yourself as though through the eyes of someone who loves you unconditionally and connect with your heart. Take a few breaths. Imagine a character, or persona, that best embodies the characteristics you shortlisted. This character is a representation of your highest self. At your most magnificent, who are you destined to be? It's OK if it feels overwhelming – enjoy acknowledging all of who you are called to be. If it doesn't come to you, take a break and have a go another day, trust that in the meantime your subconscious is working on an answer for you. Shaping your leadership identity is a lifelong commitment. Make a practice of deciding who you want to be and then make course corrections each day to show up consistent with that identity.

To bring together the various self-awareness exercises to define who you are as a leader I'm going to adapt questions used by Carlos Valdes-Dapena, an expert on high performance collaboration. In his book, *Lessons from Mars: How One Global Company Cracked the Code on High Performance Collaboration and Teamwork* (2018), he provides an exercise for aligning teams around a common purpose. I was fortunate to be trained by Carlos and have found his work on collaboration to be outstanding. The purpose questions, adapted for an individual rather than team, are:

- What? Will I give myself in service of? (habit 29, 'find your purpose')
- Why? (habit 29, 'find your purpose')
- Who? Do I have to be to deliver that purpose? (habit 9, 'shape your leadership identity')
- How? Will I play that role? (habit 8, 'achieve personal alignment', core values)

CASE STUDY: LEADERSHIP IDENTITY AS THE STANDARD OF YOUR HIGHEST SELF

What? More magic moments: creating a culture of sustainable high performance in which people can thrive and do their best work.

Why? Purpose-driven leaders. Sustainable high performance. Happier humans. Better world.

Who? An angel in plain sight (see below for explanation).

How? My core values are bold, kind, true, impact, partner and play.

Further explanation here: www.angelaarmstrong.com /manifesto

It took me a long time to claim 'an angel in plain sight' as it felt too lofty and too fluffy for the business world. I discovered it at an unmasking workshop on a leadership retreat. After two days of doing exercises to connect with my highest self, it came to me and I knew instinctively it was true. But it was several years before I became the person who was called forth that day. To me 'an angel in plain sight' means to be a force for good, with a purity of spirit for service, an infinite capacity to love, a deep trust in my intuition, being truth and light, while also being humble and grounded in the reality of the day.

Generally, your 'who' is a deeply private persona and not one that is shared publicly. I'm sharing mine here as an example, but it's not something I bring up in conversation. Knowing who you are as a leader is one of the most powerful personas you have.

See habit 11, 'decide who is driving the bus'.

– Angela Armstrong, strategic leadership partner

Benefits for you

Being true to your identity is the most effective and sustainable way to lead; it is important for our well-being, our sense of being our best selves and contributing all of who we are to the world. Your broader leadership identity increases your sense of purpose and satisfaction in your working life. When you are clear on who you are, and what you stand for, it makes decision-making simpler. You'll show up far more consistently and demonstrate your integrity (doing what you say you will do). As you show up consistently, others will notice and you'll develop a personal brand – people will know what you stand for. Often your personal brand precedes you, and opportunities will find you. Having a deep sense of identity, if it aligns with leadership strengths, gives you gravitas: you'll come across as a grounded individual who speaks their truth and who is not easily swayed, but remains open to new ideas. Having an improving trajectory as you seek personal improvement also indicates your further potential to others.

Benefits for others

When you have a strong identity as a leader, others have clarity on who you are and whether they are inspired to follow you. They can think of you as a role model, as someone of minimal influence (wallpaper!), or as an anti-role model, depending on their view of the world.

Related habits

- Use role models and mentors (habit 6)
- Achieve personal alignment (habit 8)
- Decide who is driving the bus (habit 11)
- Speak your truth (habit 26)
- Find your purpose (habit 29)

CHAPTER FOUR

Energy

This chapter is about appreciating and intelligently expending your finite energy. This book assumes that you're seeking to move your performance from 'good' to 'great'. For that to be true, you are likely already well-versed in creating energy because you consistently sleep 7 to 9 hours per night, drink 1.5 litres of fluid per day, eat a nutritious and balanced diet and move daily (doing ten thousand steps a day or 30 minutes of moderate activity). If you need to refresh your understanding with the latest thinking, see Useful Resources.

Grind. As the name suggests, 'grind' is not necessarily enjoyable – it's about 'getting it done'. Put simply, grind is what we do when we are low on reserves or doing what we know we 'should' do. Grind isn't necessarily negative – it can come from having the discipline to deliver on a commitment and show integrity. This often happens when a deadline is looming, and we've bitten off more than we can chew, or we've failed to make adequate contingency for adverse events. We rarely do our best work in this space. Short-term grind is OK but used too often it dampens our enjoyment. Positions of responsibility we once sought become unwelcome hamster wheels, and our performance drops over time.

Flow, on the other hand, is a state of concentration so focused that you are completely absorbed in a rewarding activity that is providing immediate feedback, you have a sense of personal control and ownership over the activity and you seem to lose all sense of time. To achieve flow the skill required must be perceived to be high relative to the activity, yet you remain confident that you will achieve what needs to be done while free from distraction and disruption. Flow is described by Csikszentmihalyi (2013) as an ideal state of happiness. In flow we seem to put in less effort and get far better results. Ideas come easily, decisions feel simple, time passes without us noticing and our energy levels stay high. Cardia and Miralles (2017) discuss flow as one of the secrets to a long and happy life in their studies of centenarians in Okinawa, South Japan. They link flow with 'ikigai' – why you get out of bed in the morning (See habit 29, 'find your purpose').

Much of the time we are in a more neutral state that is neither grind nor flow.

'The trick to blending work and play, lies not in
what you do, but in how you view what you do.
See work as play and see play as very important.'
  – Seth Godin, American author and former dot
    com business executive

Why it matters

The mental and physical benefits of renewal were covered
in part one: Resilience Fundamentals. Ultimately, you will
have reserves that you can draw on to respond to adverse
events and to say 'yes' to opportunities that excite you.
Having excess energy fuels bigger ambitions – you can't
have World-changing influence when you can barely keep
your eyes open at 9pm on a Friday night. Having positive
energy also draws others to us, giving us more opportunity
to influence.

This chapter includes the following habits:

10. Do energy accounting – understand which activities
    give you energy, and which deplete you so you can
    schedule activities to have consistent high energy.

11. Decide who is driving the bus – how to re-energise
    yourself on demand to show up powerfully in critical
    moments.

12. Maximise value with minimal effort – how to
    intelligently expend your energy to maximise results.

13. Manage your boundaries – how to determine and
    communicate your boundaries to negotiate work
    requests and other demands.

Habit 10: Do Energy Accounting

Recognising which activities (or people) consume energy, give us energy or are fairly neutral, means that we can make better informed scheduling decisions to have more consistent energy (and therefore productivity) levels. Managing your energy turns diary management on its head, because not all time is equal from an energy perspective. When we are in 'grind', a minute can feel like an hour, when we are in 'flow' the opposite is true. We achieve more and perform more consistently when we manage our energy, not our time.

Different people are energised and depleted by different things. For example, someone with a natural predisposition towards detailed tasks will find doing an in-depth analysis either neutral or energising, while someone who is predisposed towards big ideas and concepts will probably feel depleted by the same activity. Playing to our strengths is less tiring than developing new skills and it's also when we most often experience flow. Acting outside of our natural preference is tiring, as we have to make a conscious effort. Feeling depleted can lead to 'over-extended' behaviours; for example, being rude when we are ordinarily polite and respectful. Psychometric assessments can provide insights into our natural strengths and help inform our energy accounting practice. See www.TheResilienceClub.co.uk for further information.

EXERCISE: WHAT ENERGISES YOU?

Write a list of all the activities you do regularly.

Next to each activity, mark a '+' for activities that give you energy, a '–' for activities that drain you and leave any others unmarked as neutral.

Allocate activities you repeatedly do to your different 'batteries': physical, mental, emotional, spiritual. See the examples in the table for some ideas.

	Depletes	*Neutral*	*Energises*
Physical	Sitting still for hours	Walk and talk at lunch	Dancing
Mental	Filling in my expenses	Planning my week	Delivering training
Emotional	Revisiting old arguments	Routine back-office tasks	Coaching, connecting one-to-one
Spiritual	Doing lots of similar tasks	Meeting new people	Variety, travel

EXERCISE: SCHEDULE YOUR ENERGY (NOT YOUR TIME)

Notice whether you give most of your energy at work or home. What would you like the balance to be? How can you move towards that ideal?

Where do you need to review your scheduling to ensure that there is adequate time for renewal or energising activity? Do you regularly book lots of activities that deplete you on the same day? For example, if doing all your admin activity in one go on a Friday makes you miserable intersperse admin with activities you find energising.

It's the thing you do, before the thing you do, that provides the energy! For example, if exercise energises you and you've exercised before going to the office then you'll have plenty of energy for your first task of the day. Your energy at the start of the first task is high because of the exercise; whether your energy remains high by the time you've finished the task depends on whether that task is one that energises or depletes you, which in turn determines how much energy is available to the next task.

We all have a natural biorhythm: some people are 'night owls' while others are 'early birds'. Noticing how our energy changes through the day can help us with scheduling activity. For example, on office days, I prefer to do routine tasks and social contact in the morning and complex solo tasks in the afternoon. Of course, we can't always organise our days to suit our preferences, but at least knowing what they are means that when the opportunity arises, we make the most of it. We can condition ourselves to routines that don't fit with our natural biorhythm (for example, shift workers) but doing so further depletes the energy we have available.

You might also find it informative to look through the list of habits and see if it prompts a thought about your biggest energy drains. Clients often tell me that they regularly bite off more than they can chew (see habit 24), deprioritise the basics (see start of chapter four, 'Energy'), beat themselves up (see habit 27) or spend time around people who drain their energy (see habit 7).

Benefits for you

When you are more aware of your fluctuating energy levels, and what energises or depletes you, you can schedule your activities so that you always have some spare capacity, which helps you to feel more resilient and enables you to spend more time in flow. Creating or contributing to a team of people with diverse psychometric preferences and skills enables collaboration that makes the most of individual talent and allows people to operate in flow.

Benefits for others

Anticipating the week ahead enables you to deliver on your work commitments, benefiting your colleagues. It also benefits your friends, as you don't renege on social engagements at short notice because you're too tired.

Related habits

- Design your peer group (habit 7)
- Decide who is driving the bus (habit 11)

Habit 11: Decide Who Is Driving the Bus

Humans have complex personalities; this habit is about bringing forth different energies (or personas) from our personality to suit different occasions. Personas often reflect our different roles in life. Role-based personas that express the best of who we are might include:

- Ambitious individual
- Progressive leader
- Present and playful parent
- Fun-loving friend
- Sex god/goddess
- Nurturing family member

More generic personas may include:

- Change-maker
- Kick-ass warrior

You probably already switch between moderate versions of your personas without doing it consciously (for example, during your commute). Now imagine that your total identity is like a minibus being driven along the road of life, and all your personas are passengers. This habit is about deciding which persona is driving the bus (i.e. your thoughts, feelings and behaviours) in that moment. By consciously deciding who is driving the bus and summoning the most powerful and aligned version of that persona, you can deliberately show up as the best version of you when the occasion demands it. First you need to define the persona. The following exercise uses a technique from NLP (neurolinguistic programming) called anchoring. An earlier version of anchoring, based only on touch, first appeared in Grinder and Bandler (1979).

EXERCISE: CREATE AN ANCHOR FOR YOUR BEST PERSONAS

If you want to do this activity on your own, you'll need a device that can record voice memos. Otherwise, do it as a pair and capture key words for each other.

1. Start by thinking of one positive persona you already recognise within yourself – one that you'd benefit from being able to summon at will.

2. Cast yourself back to the time when you exemplified that persona. Close your eyes if that's easier. Fully immerse yourself in that persona: relive that specific moment, re-experience what if felt like to be that persona, stand in the posture that persona would use. This technique doesn't work if you describe the persona as if you are *observing* yourself; you must fully *re-experience* that persona.

3. Describe what it feels like to be the best version of that persona, embellishing if necessary, and saying the words out loud. Make the recall as rich as possible using the prompts in the table. Aim for at least twelve words for each of body, focus and words.

---

4. **Body** How do you hold yourself when you are being this persona?
What does it feel like physically?
What smell or touch is associated with this persona?
Examples: standing tall, strong, relaxed, smells fresh, feels soft

---

Focus What are you focusing on when you are being this persona?
What emotions are you feeling?
What do you notice about your surroundings?
Examples: possibilities, future, solutions, confident, congruent, sunny

---

Words What are you saying to yourself when you are being this
persona?

What are others saying to you?

What else can you hear? Music? What song?

Examples: I can, I will, you inspire me, wow, friends cheering

---

5. While you're still richly re-experiencing yourself in
this persona, give this persona a nickname – whatever
pops into your head. Giving your persona a distinct
identity provides a handle that encapsulates all that
rich remembering.

6. What colour do you associate with this persona?

7. What gesture do you associate with this persona? Do
the gesture while you are still re-experiencing yourself
in this persona.

8. Take a few minutes to relax and return to a more
neutral persona.

9. Deliberately summon the persona you just re-
experienced (see tips below) to prove to yourself that
you can change the driver of the bus at will.

10. Repeat steps 2–8 of this exercise two or three times
per week for each persona. Week 1 should focus on
your first persona, week 2 on the next, and so on.
That will anchor the best version of each persona and
make it easier to summon them later.

TOP TIPS: SUMMON A SPECIFIC PERSONA

When you need to summon a persona to drive the bus, you can say something like 'C'mon, <nickname>, it's time for you to drive, let's go!' and the work you did to anchor the sensation of showing up as that persona will kick in.

To remind you of the persona you want to summon throughout the day:

- Wear an item of clothing in the colour you associate with that persona
- Wear the fragrance you associate with that persona
- Listen to the song you identified during the re-experiencing exercise (for example, on your way to a meeting)
- Do the gesture that you did during the anchoring exercise

Most people will only need to define a handful of frequently used personas to show up more powerfully and deliberately as the best version of themselves. It requires a little effort upfront to do the anchoring exercise, but you'll be able to call on the persona for a lifetime and it will get easier each time you do it. As time passes, you might let a persona gather dust or decide to create a new one – our personality evolves gently over time.

Our most powerful personas draw together our physical, mental, emotional and spiritual energy. When we work with absolute certainty towards goals that are personally aligned for us (habit 8, 'achieve personal alignment') we exude an energy that others can sense and are drawn to. With this energy you won't take no for an answer and you'll find or make a way to overcome any obstacles in your path to where you want to be. These moments may be few and far between, but when we create them, we can move mountains.

EMPOWERING BELIEF
Resourceful people get resources.

CASE STUDY: FLEXING YOUR AUTHENTIC STYLE TO ACHIEVE POSITIVE OUTCOMES

I'm the co-founder and sales director of a rapidly growing legal services firm with 100 employees and 15 franchises. I naturally have a lot of energy and creativity which enables me to inspire other business owners and talk passionately about our purpose of 'keeping families together'. There are also times when I have to be more grounded when I'm talking to people who like detail and thoroughness – the lifeblood of our company! For example, being able to deliberately decide how I want to show up enables me to get the outcomes we need for both winning, and signing, a new partner practice. Importantly, I don't feel like I'm being inauthentic; I have both characters in me – I just decide who is driving the bus.

– Mike Simpson, Owner and Sales Director, Right Legal Group

It takes deliberate effort and energy to change the driver of the bus, which is why most people don't do it at all, and even those that use this habit do it inconsistently. However, you do have a choice. Sometimes you have to choose to apply extra effort to get what you want. Pick the moments when you need to really 'show up' to life with your best. If you're surrounded by colleagues who are dour and who sap your energy, it's worth looking at changing your peer group (or spending less time with them) instead of continually pepping yourself up by changing driver.

Benefits for you

By being able to deliberately summon your most effective persona for a given situation, you'll feel more in control of your emotions, and consistently meet your commitments because you no longer have to 'wait until you're in the mood' to get things done. You'll show up more often aligned to the highest standard you set for yourself. You'll be less prone to anxiety or depression – or at least you won't stay there for long, because now you know how to put a more resourceful persona in the driving seat.

Benefits for others

People around you will have confidence that you will show up as your best self when the occasion demands it. For example, to represent their views to senior leaders. While aware of your different personas people will still recognise your core values as a common foundation. When your character is regularly demonstrated, others don't waste energy second-guessing your reaction – they know what to expect.

Related habits

- Design your peer group (habit 7)
- Shape your leadership identity (habit 9)
- Do energy accounting (habit 10)
- Express your true spirit (habit 21)

Habit 12: Maximise Value with Minimal Effort

This habit combines three themes to help you deliver maximum value for the effort you put in: the 80/20 rule, 'progress, not perfect' and multiplier effect.

The 80/20 rule

This power-law probability distribution was originally called the Pareto principle. In the nineteenth century, Vilfredo Pareto observed that 80% of the land in Italy was owned by about 20% of the population. The concept was more recently popularised by Richard Koch (Koch, 2014), who applied it to business economics and called it the 80/20 rule. Koch states that for almost everything in life, we can derive 80% of the results from 20% of the effort *when we focus on the elements of a task that add the highest value*. For ease of comparison, let's assume that you're not applying this rule at all currently, if you then started to apply the 80/20 rule to everything you do – just 1 day of effort (20% of the working week) could get you 4-days' worth of results (80% of the working week). What else could you do with all the time you just freed up?

> **EMPOWERING BELIEF**
> There is always time enough
> for my highest priorities.

When we expend effort beyond the high-value 20%, it suffers from the law of diminishing returns: that is, the first 20% gets us 80% of the result, but the next 10% only moves us a small percentage further forward. The returns get worse the closer we get to 'perfect' or 100%.

You know it's true in your own life. Need to write a report? You can type out a first draft that contains all the key messages (80% return) pretty quickly (20% effort), but to hone it into a work of art takes considerably more effort. It's likely that as a result of that extra effort, you'll only find a handful of key messages that you didn't capture on the first pass. That's not to say that the report shouldn't be honed... but does it need to be you who does it? Can you delegate it to someone on a lower pay grade or with a different skill set, and then step back in to review and finalise? Can you deliver 80% of the value via a video call (20% effort), rather than the overhead of travelling to a different location to meet someone face-to-face? Can the 20% of effort to create a 'rough order of magnitude' estimate give you 80% or 'good enough' information to make a decision before narrowing down to a few options to evaluate in more detail?

By keeping the 80/20 rule in mind and delegating appropriately, we also 'act our pay grade' by focusing our effort only on those activities through which we add the most value. Which activities require your highest value? Which activities can only be done by you?

Progress, not perfect

'Progress, not perfect' is about giving yourself emotional 'permission' to follow the 80/20 approach. If you're carrying out life-saving surgery or providing the final set of accounts to the auditors then 'absolutely accurate' is a reasonable aspiration, but for most tasks and activities you can let 'good enough' be good enough. You already understand that due to the law of diminishing returns, chasing perfection is squandering energy that you could use elsewhere to generate more value for yourself and others. If you recognise yourself as a perfectionist, give yourself permission to deliver 'good enough' solutions for a while. See that other people barely notice, and if they do then the difference isn't worth shouting about or they are making a valuable contribution – great! You might not have come up with that addition anyway; they are looking at it with fresh eyes and from a different perspective, and their contribution is in their 20% of effort – an easy value-add.

What else could you do to add more value or enjoy life more with the time you've saved by delivering 80% of the result for 20% of the effort? Experimenting with 'progress, not perfect' and noticing that the sky doesn't fall in will help you make the emotional shift to a 'progress, not perfect' way of life, which will lower your anxiety level and help you plough through the tasks on your to-do list. If you come out in a cold sweat just thinking about this suggestion, it might be worth doing some research on a schema called 'unrelenting standards' and finding a trained counsellor near you to uncover where that resistance is coming from. I did just that. It's genuinely life-changing, as it allows you to pursue projects you'd never otherwise have tried.

> **INCONVENIENT TRUTH**
> Some of the pressure you feel is created by your own high standards.

CASE STUDY: RECOGNISING WHEN NEAR ENOUGH IS GOOD ENOUGH

I am an engineer by profession. Overseeing huge smart infrastructure projects requires a high degree of precision because people's lives are at risk. However, I realised that I was taking my tendency for perfectionism a little too far when I spent half a day at the weekend assessing the pros and cons of various models of washing machines. Now, in circumstances when a 'good enough' solution will do, I set a timescale for making a decision and a few criteria for a good enough solution before I start analysing options. By letting go of everything having to be so perfect I'm putting myself under less strain.

– Ritchie Burcombe, Project Director

Multiplier effect

I am a big fan of NET (no extra time) and VAT (value-added time). You can practise many of the habits in this book safely while you are doing other things that you need to do anyway (NET). For example, you can practise the 80/20 rule, and habit 10, 'do energy accounting' while you're planning your work. You can practise other habits in combination, so you maximise the benefits you're gaining from the same time (VAT). For example, you can take a short walk in the fresh air with a mentor to have lunch away from your desk. That's four resilience benefits in the time it takes to do one (exercise, downtime, mentor, minimise digital distractions).

Benefits for you

By expending the minimum valuable effort, you show competence in 'acting your pay grade' and release more time and energy for other things. Make your mantra at work 'get in, get it done, get out!' Even if you love your work, you'll have time and energy to create a life you love too – and you'll return to the workplace in higher spirits because of it.

Benefits for others

You'll have more time and energy for others. A minimum valuable effort approach also encourages collaboration, where everyone contributes their time and talents effectively and feels valued. Others will enjoy working with you: all work and no play grinds us down and lowers our energy – who wants to work with that person?

Related habits

- Prioritise your sphere of control (habit 1)
- Direct your focus (habit 2)
- Solve the root cause of the problem (habit 3)
- Do energy accounting (habit 10)

Habit 13: Manage Your Boundaries

This habit has three parts: communicate your boundaries, say 'no' constructively and say 'hell, yes'. Managing the demands on our time is a core skill for managing our resilience. By assessing requests at source, we become more deliberate about what we say 'yes' to, and that makes us more reliable professionally and more grounded emotionally.

Communicate your boundaries

A boundary is what we deem to be OK or not OK for us. For example, working an hour longer on a weekday to get something finished is OK by me, but taking work calls while I'm on holiday is not. To set boundaries, we first have to know what is important to us (see habit 8, 'achieve personal alignment'). We then have to experiment with establishing a few personal life rules that guide our decision-making to protect those values. Once established, our life rules make day-to-day decision-making in those areas faster and simpler. We have to communicate our boundaries, rather than expect that other people are telepathic. For example, a simple rule that supports the core value of 'family' could be expressed as 'I *value* family time, so I *need* focused connection, and I will *honour* that need by having no devices at the dinner table.' It can be helpful to practice saying 'I'll get back to you' or 'I can't take that on right now' when no one is present, so that you get used to saying it.

Of course, setting boundaries is one thing; holding to them when other people would like us to behave differently is another. This requires commitment and the courage to speak our truth (see habit 26, 'speak your truth'). To stay true to ourselves, we have to risk disappointing others. Having boundaries is not about being selfish: when we are aligned, and we protect our renewal time, we have more energy to contribute to others. We let other people know our boundaries, and by and large we aim to interact with people who respect those boundaries.

> **EMPOWERING BELIEF**
> Self-care is not selfish: I cannot
> pour from an empty cup.

At work, our boundaries have to be informed by an employment contract, so we select or negotiate work arrangements that fit with our values. For example, Euan Murray, the Scottish rugby union international, contracted that as a Christian he would not play on Sundays. That meant he was not available for a crucial 2011 World Cup group game against Argentina.

Say 'no' constructively

In workshops I often introduce this topic by stating that 'No' is a full sentence and pause while the idea is absorbed. Typically, we prefer to offer some sort of explanation or follow-up comment, but we shouldn't feel that we have to. That said, we can soften the message and offer other ways in which we can add value that require less effort on our part (see habit 12, 'maximise value with minimal effort').

> 'Daring to set boundaries is about having the courage to love ourselves, even when we risk disappointing others.'
> – Brené Brown

Saying 'no' to a new commitment also means that you're honouring your existing commitments and ensuring that you'll be able to devote quality time to them. Saying 'no' does not make you uncooperative or a poor team player, but a solid, dedicated individual who stands their ground and recognises the areas in which their talents are best contributed. When we spread ourselves too thinly, no good comes of it – for us or for others. If you never say 'no' then your 'yes' has no value, because it is taken for granted. Maybe you feel taken for granted too.

Here is how to professionally say 'no' in a way that adds value to the person asking but doesn't compromise your boundaries.

Delay	Create delay between the request and your reply so you can consider it
Consider	Capabilities: Is the request a good fit for your role, abilities and grade?
	Priorities: Does the request fit with your current priorities?
	Benefits: Can you see a long-term benefit in answer to 'What's in it for me?'
	Minimum valuable effort: What 20% effort can I offer to get an 80% result? What other resources can I signpost? Is there someone else who could help? Can I provide a previous paper as an example? (See habit 12, 'maximise value with minimal effort')
	Timing: If I am the right person to help, can I negotiate the timing?
Reply	Say no, offer headline information from your consideration
	Negotiate timing or signpost other ways the person can resolve their request
	Share your relevant boundaries so they know what's non-negotiable

I have been on many promotion boards that have decided *not* to promote highly capable, ambitious and dedicated people but instead mentor them until they learn to say 'no' appropriately. Well-managed companies don't want their high performers to burn out when taking on greater responsibilities, because sustainable high performance ultimately yields greater value. As you progress your career, you'll spend more time on strategic, slow-burn activities like building partnerships and anticipating the future. To create space for those activities when more pressing operational demands are being made, you need to understand the value that the strategic activities add, and you need to have enough courage to say 'no' to immediate needs... and immediate reward or gratification. Occasionally we have to 'muck in' to get the job done but do so consciously rather than as a reflex action.

CASE STUDY: SAYING 'NO' LEADING TO PROMOTION

I am passionate about the work that I do, and I believe that we can achieve more when we collaborate. At times, I felt that by being so willing to support others I was being pulled in all directions, and I didn't have enough hours in the day. At the same time, I was looking to progress my career and taking on extracurricular effort to impress. When I realised my approach wasn't working, I started managing my boundaries better, saying no to some requests and being more focused on where I could add value, asking for more clarity or support where I needed it. As a result, I was fully committed to the things I said yes to, still able to offer targeted support to colleagues and feel much more in control of my remit. And I got promoted, in part because my manager realised, I had the skills to navigate the additional demands!

– Fiona Shelton, Dean of Students and Head of the Centre for Excellence in Learning and Teaching, University of Derby

Say 'hell, yes'

More than a yes, a 'hell, yes' is something you are keen to do, which energises you and feels congruent for you. You can reply in an instant because it immediately resonates – a 'hell, yes' doesn't need thinking through – even if you don't yet know how you'll make it happen. Look for ways to turn a request that you would ordinarily reply 'yes' to into a 'hell, yes' to upgrade your life! What would you need to add to the request to turn it from a 'yes' to a 'hell, yes'? Family outing? Yes. To somewhere you've wanted to go for ages? Hell, yes. Meet with colleagues for a drink after work? Yes. Someone you've wanted to gain access to is also going? Hell, yes. Volunteering for a day? Yes. Opportunity to grow by interacting with a more diverse set of people? Hell, yes.

Ask for help

We are all talented at different things and have different life experience, so we all have something to offer each other. When we are playing to our strengths, we can add value with minimal effort (see habit 12, 'maximise value with minimal effort'), so it doesn't take a big leap of logic to make faster progress by collaborating with others to get things done efficiently. To do that, we need to be able to ask for help in a 'capable adult' way that doesn't come across as passive or needy and accept that help graciously. Contrary to popular belief, no one is telepathic: ask specifically for what you need.

> **EMPOWERING BELIEF**
> It's OK to ask for help.

When we ask others to support us, we also give them tacit permission to ask us for support at another time. What goes around comes around, and you'll help them another day.

> **INCONVENIENT TRUTH**
> Sustained high performance is a team sport.

TOP TIPS: ASKING FOR HELP

- Understand when you need help
- Be specific about what you need
- Ask someone who can help you
- Create value for the person you are asking
- Ask with the energy and expectation that they will say 'yes'
- Refine your request and ask again, or ask someone else, until you get what you need.

Benefits for you

When you set boundaries and are better able to ask for, and graciously accept, support from others, you do not feel resentment (from saying 'yes' when you meant 'no'), you build your self-respect and deliver maximum value for time.

You also make a significant contribution to turning high performance into sustainable high performance.

Benefits for others

Showing up in this 'capable adult' way builds respect with colleagues and others. They're actually more likely to ask you for help, as they know you'll say 'no' if you can't. When you first take care of yourself, you have more to give to others, contributing to a sense of compassion and social support.

Related habits

- Achieve personal alignment (habit 8)
- Maximise value with minimal effort (habit 12)
- Accept what is (habit 14)
- Be vulnerable and surrender (habit 17)
- Speak your truth (habit 26)

CHAPTER FIVE

Emotions

Being able to manage your emotions effectively is a central skill in your resilience toolkit. Without it, we can feel like our emotions are running away with us. There are only two base emotions, love and fear, all others are variants, and we cannot feel both at the same time, so in each moment we get to choose love or fear (Kubler-Ross and Kessler, 2014). Both fear and love can feel big and scary when we feel unable to control them, and there are two typical fear-driven reactions. The first is staying well within our comfort zone, playing small, so that we do not invoke strong emotions. The second is 'soldiering on' but numbing or denying all emotions. We cannot only numb our negative emotions (such as disgust, sadness and anger); we reduce our emotional range on both sides, so we miss out on the positive emotions too (such as joy, trust and acceptance). Instead, we can choose to come from love and acknowledge that *all* emotions are part of the richness of the human experience and learn how to embrace and navigate all of them.

Why it matters

The long-term effects of stress on your body was covered in the earlier chapter 'stress is a choice'. Positive moods are often associated with increased creativity, problem-solving, mental flexibility and efficiency in decision-making and contribute to optimism. Low moods negatively affect how we process information, our ability to focus, and our ability to make considered decisions, and they create a pessimistic bias. On the upside, a low mood increases our ability to pay attention to detail and ask probing questions. People buy people, we are not robots, it's necessary to appropriately express emotions in the workplace firstly to acknowledge that you are a human being and secondly because emotions are 50% of your ability to influence 'hearts and minds'. Your ability to manage your emotions also significantly impacts the quality of the relationships you can have with others.

Emotional stability dampens your physiological response so there are fewer stress hormones in your bloodstream, enabling you to think clearly under pressure. Emotional self-management gives you the freedom to experience and enjoy the full range of human emotions while having a sense of control, which feels like a life fully lived. It also means that you are less likely to say or do something in the heat of the moment that you later regret, which could damage an important relationship permanently. When you have emotional mastery, it's easier to influence others by expressing emotions (for example, to sell a vision you truly believe in), and they will have a greater sense of emotional safety and feel able to bring you good news and bad news, knowing that you'll have a proportionate response.

Daniel Goleman is a prominent expert in the field of emotional intelligence. He describes emotional intelligence as comprising four elements: self-awareness, self-management, social awareness and relationship management. As this book is focused on habits that are entirely within our control, this chapter focuses on the first two: self-awareness (habit 15, 'process emotions as data') and self-management (the other habits).

This chapter includes the following habits:

14. Accept what is – letting go emotionally of things that are outside your control

15. Process emotions as data – increase your awareness of your emotions and what wisdom they hold so that you can take the learning and let the emotion pass

16. Avoid vicious cycles – interrupt thought patterns that lead to low mood or ongoing distress

17. Be vulnerable and surrender – releasing internal tension and learning to listen to your body

18. Work through the emotional change curve – there is a typical pattern of emotions that accompany change, learn to surf them like a pro

Habit 14: Accept What Is

If you read habit 1, 'prioritise your sphere of control', you will know that some things are outside your control, so they are not worth your **mental** energy to seek solutions. This habit is about emotionally accepting that some things are outside your control so that you don't use unnecessary **emotional** energy.

A simple example is realising (ideally ahead of time) that you can't finish a piece of work before the deadline. Instead of sticking your head in the sand and denying the inevitable awareness of your shortcomings, accept the reality, and renegotiate the deadline. Spending emotional energy wishing the facts were different won't help. Suppressing the emotion (see habit 15, 'process emotions as data') won't help either. Humans are fallible: we don't get it right all the time; a lesson in humility every now and then does you no harm.

Other people's decisions, words and behaviours are outside your control. It's an important distinction that *you do not need to accept the poor behaviour* and there may be consequences for the behaviour.

If you are experiencing emotions about things that are not within your sphere of control, pause and get curious about what you would have to believe to be involved emotionally in how someone else lives their life. It is often a projection of your own behaviour standards – for example, thinking that someone shouldn't do something which goes against your beliefs and standards.

Instead of focusing on what someone else is, or is not, doing – the bit that's outside your control – focus on accepting emotionally that they are self-determined individuals making choices that are different from yours. It is not serving you or helping them for you to be emotionally embroiled and fighting fire with fire is rarely a route to swift resolution.

When you accept that their actions are outside your control, you remain calmer and you can think more clearly. By demonstrating emotional self-management, you open the possibility of explaining to them how to do the same… after their emotions have become less intense and if it's appropriate.

Unless we ask, we cannot know what thought process generated someone else's actions. Their intentions may be well-intended, but their actions misguided. We are all doing the best we can with the resources available to us in this moment, and when we know better, we do better. No one gets it right all the time.

This habit is useful at work during periods of change, when often our first response is to want a level of certainty about what is changing and how it will affect us. By the very nature of change, the detail is being clarified as we go along, and full information is not currently available – so certainty about the solution is outside our sphere of control. An example follows.

The key author on this topic is Byron Katie. In her book *Loving What Is*, she offers a simple yet powerful process of inquiry, called The Work, which teaches you how to identify and question the thoughts that are hurting you, and how to address the cause of your problems with clarity. In its most basic form, The Work consists of four questions and the turnarounds.

EXAMPLE: ORGANISATIONAL CHANGE

Step 1 – Write down what you perceive to be wrong.	I need to know exactly what will happen next
Step 2 – Ask the four questions:	
1. Is it true?	Mostly
2. Can you absolutely know that it's true?	OK, no, I get that there's a lot that is still unknown at this stage and I can only know the direction of travel now.
3. How do you react, what happens, when you think that thought?	When I need to know exactly what will happen next and leadership are not providing answers, I get suspicious, anxious and entrenched in my position – I resist change until I feel more certain.
4. Who would you be without the thought?	I'd be more willing to get involved with shaping the solution or accept that it's an evolving picture and stay aware until I'm called upon, while getting on with what I must do now.
Step 3 – Find the turnarounds.	'I need to know exactly what will happen next' becomes 'I don't need to know exactly what will happen next'.

The turnaround is an opportunity to experience the opposite of what you originally believed. Then find specific, genuine examples of how each turnaround is as true as, or truer than, your original thought.

This habit is not about 'rolling over' and taking whatever life dishes out. It's about expending your energy intelligently on the things you can control and emotionally letting go of the things that you can't.

EXERCISE: ACCEPT WHAT IS

What emotions are you currently experiencing related to something outside your control? How would it be if you could acknowledge the situation as simply 'interesting' without getting immersed in the drama? Use the examples above to guide you in accepting what is.

Everything you need to do The Work (on a belief or on a situation) to transform your life is available free of charge on Byron Katie's website, http://thework.com/en/do-work. The website also provides a link to a free mobile phone app and a free Helpline to support you.

Benefits for you

Emotionally accepting things outside your control conserves your energy and allows your head and heart to return to alignment, restoring a sense of internal peace. When you feel more at peace you can be more productive, which protects time to spend on your other priorities. Emotional self-management means you are less likely to say or do things you later regret and increases your gravitas as a leader.

Benefits for others

You accept others as rational, capable human beings who are making self-determined decisions based on their core values, regardless of whether or not you perceive their beliefs or actions to be 'right'. By remaining emotionally neutral, you 'hold space' for them to feel heard and process their emotions so that they can decide what to do next. Leaders who are emotionally more stable show others how to moderate emotionally charged debates so that the team can quickly return to focus on the task at hand.

Related habits

- Prioritise your sphere of control (habit 1)
- Achieve personal alignment (habit 8)
- Process emotions as data (habit 15)
- Work through the emotional change curve (habit 18)

Habit 15: Process Emotions as Data

Now that we've cut down the number of things to get emotional about (see habit 1, 'prioritise your sphere of control' and habit 14, 'accept what is'), let's look at how we can process the ones that are meant for us. Emotions themselves are neither good nor bad: they just are. Our emotions are biological triggers that alert us when all is not as we'd like it to be. If we stay open and curious about our emotions, we can become consciously aware of them without judging them. We can identify and label the emotion, and then hit the 'pause' button to allow our prefrontal cortex to process the emotion intellectually, letting us discover what wisdom that emotion is trying to impart to us, learn the lesson, decide if and how we want to react, and let the emotion flow through. We're not supposed to hang on to emotions, but some, like grief, tend to linger longer than others because we have more emotional processing to do.

Notice, identify and label your emotions

In English there are around four hundred words for different emotions, yet most people experience only fifteen to twenty frequently that they can identify and label in the moment when they are experiencing them. 'I feel happy' and 'I feel sad' are the two phrases that we often use first, but there are many more (see Appendix D for a list of words for emotions).

EXERCISE: NOTICE YOUR EMOTIONAL RANGE

1. Notice and label your emotions at regular intervals throughout the day. Record what emotion you are feeling and what activity you are doing at the time.
2. Keep a log for a week, recording at least five times each day (set an electronic reminder). This recording will give you a picture of which emotions you experience most often and what your current trigger and response habits are. Are you more often 'up' or 'down'?

Moderate your emotions

Extending your vocabulary around emotions not only helps you to articulate how you are feeling to others (see habit 26, 'speak your truth') but also enables you to experience a broader range of emotions because the label you give an emotion influences how strongly you feel it. If your only options are 'frustrated' or 'angry' then you'll usually experience emotions of that intensity when triggered. If you have a broader range, you'll have more options for moderating your biological reaction to better reflect the intensity of the trigger. For example, other options for feelings experienced as frustration or anger could include: 'disrespected', 'disappointed', 'provoked', 'annoyed', 'sceptical', 'dismissive', 'let down', 'humiliated' or 'mad'. It might sound daft, but it works (for a deeper understanding, see habit 16, 'avoid vicious cycles'). Emojis just don't cut it for sharing the complexity of our emotions or moderating their intensity; words do.

EXERCISE: EXTEND YOUR EMOTIONAL FLEXIBILITY

1. Take two minutes and write down all the words for emotions you experience.

2. Take another two minutes and add other emotion words you know of but don't experience.

3. Boost your vocabulary by looking in Appendix D or typing 'wheel of emotions' into a search engine.

4. Review your previous log of emotions. Is there a different word that is closer to the intensity of the emotion you originally noted?

5. Anticipate the week ahead. If there is an event in your diary that previously triggered a strong emotion for you, 'pre-book' the emotion you'd prefer to experience and add a reminder in your calendar alongside the event.

6. After the event reflect on how you responded emotionally and what you're pleased with or would do differently next time. Remember, you can only control *your response* to the trigger event.

Sleep also has a role to play in helping us sort through our emotions from the day: if we don't get enough, we tend to be more emotional. This reality is also why it's often better to 'sleep on it' and come back to a discussion rather than let things get heated and risk saying something that you might later regret.

Process your emotions

Processing our emotions, like cleaning the house, is best done little and often. If you're currently an emotionally responsive person or addicted to drama (hormones) you may pick up several strong emotions throughout the day. First, identify and label your individual emotions to avoid emotional overwhelm and unpack them one at a time.

EXERCISE: UNPACK YOUR EMOTIONS

To unpack your emotions one at a time, ask yourself:

1. Where did this emotion come from?

2. Is the emotion I am feeling proportionate to the trigger?

3. What is interesting about my response to that trigger? What can I learn?

4. Say 'thank you' to the emotion for the insight it created and let it go.

Express, don't repress, your emotions

When we repress our emotions instead of expressing them, we're storing up trouble for later. The biological response goes on in the background, creating nagging thoughts or manifesting as physical deterioration. Ultimately, our biological emotion and associated hormonal responses are trying to tell us something; if we don't pay attention willingly, eventually our body stops us in our tracks – usually through illness – until we do give our emotions some attention. Often giving our emotions attention means sorting through some memories or reconciling some unaligned thoughts. At this point our emotions can pour forth with the intensity of a pressure cooker, and a counsellor will likely be the person who is best able to guide you on how to process your emotions. The tipping point that unleashes these emotions may seem trivial compared with the response. Stubbing our toe or narrowly avoiding an accident can be the 'straw that breaks the camel's back', but the root cause is the unresolved tension that comes from not attending to the emotion when it arose. Express, don't repress, your emotions.

There are ways to express intense emotions safely, in a way that doesn't harm you or anyone else. Examples include crying or having a rant alone in a parked car. The noise doesn't carry too far, and you get some of the intensity out of your system, so you only need to deal with the residual emotions afterwards.

Once you are more practised at identifying, labelling, moderating and processing your emotions, you'll be better able to express them to others (see habit 26, 'speak your truth').

Benefits for you

You feel more in control of your emotions and can experience a full range of emotional expression, and still have emotional intelligence. It feels like a life fully lived – you're no longer numbing out. You'll also be better able to influence and persuade others because people buy in to things with their head and heart; if you give purely rational explanations, you're trying to influence using half measures.

Benefits for others

Your emotional control will give others a sense of emotional safety. People feel more able to approach you about potentially emotive subjects, or in a crisis, as they know they can rely on your proportionate and clear-headed response. When you express your emotions appropriately, others see you as human; you'll appear more approachable and they'll find it easier to make a connection.

Related habits

- Accept what is (habit 14)
- Work through the emotional change curve (habit 18)
- Speak your truth (habit 26)

Habit 16: Avoid Vicious Cycles

In 'stress is a choice' we discussed that your conversations are contagious – what you think about generates a chemical response in your body, either the 'fight, flight or freeze' response or the 'rest and digest' response – the same is true of your internal dialogue. We tend to have unconscious thought patterns that we repeat often, and we can get in a negative (vicious) cycle that leads to low moods from time to time if we don't know how to prevent it. This habit is about interrupting a vicious cycle when you spot it so that you can return to a neutral emotion, or even better create a virtuous (mood uplifting) cycle.

This model from cognitive behavioural therapy explains that our thoughts drive our results, so what we choose to think about is important.

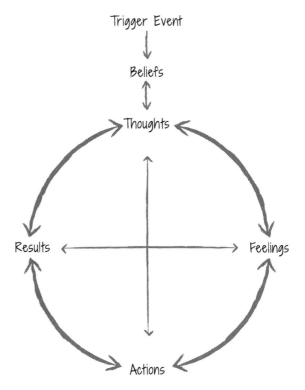

FIG. 5.1: COGNITIVE BEHAVIOURAL THERAPY
(BELIEFS DRIVE OUR RESULTS)

Your first response to an event that could trigger stress is to have a thought about the event, your beliefs inform your thoughts, your thoughts drive your feelings, your feelings drive your actions, and those actions generate results. The results you get inform your beliefs, and around you go again. Many of us know this process by the term 'vicious cycle'; with a small interruption it can also become a 'virtuous cycle'. You'll also notice that all the elements (thoughts, feelings, actions and results) influence each other – which is great, because it means that we can interrupt the cycle at any point.

Here's an example of a single trigger leading to different outcomes depending on the initial thought.

	Vicious Cycle	Virtuous Cycle
Trigger event	You were caught in traffic and arrive late for an important meeting.	
Thought / belief	Typical, why is there always a jam when I'm in a rush? (Focus is outside your control)	I could have left home earlier. (Focus is within your control)
Feeling	Frustrated with the volume of traffic and slow progress. Get increasingly anxious about what others will think about you.	Disappointed. I won't create a good first impression. Accept I can't change the past and return to neutral emotion.
Actions	Apologise for being late, blame the traffic, take some time to calm down emotionally and only add value just as meeting ends.	Apologise for being late, acknowledge that I could have left home earlier, deliver value in the room and impress client.
Results / body	Lateness negatively impacted my mood and meeting outcome. Your brain perceives ongoing threat and your system continues to release cortisol.	Lateness professionally handled, meeting outcome still achieved. Your brain does not feel under threat so the 'rest and digest' cycle initiates.
Reinforcing thought	The world is out to get me.	I'm usually on time; I'll allow more contingency next time.

When we are in a vicious cycle, it can be tricky to think our way out of it. These tips change your biochemistry and dampen your stress response, making it easier to interrupt the vicious cycle in the moment.

TOP TIPS: INTERRUPTING THE VICIOUS CYCLE IN THE EXAMPLE

- Thoughts: let someone who will be in the meeting know you are running late to help you 'let go' of the fact that you'll be late.
- Feelings: do something nice for someone else: this releases oxytocin, the 'hug drug', In your car: smiling at someone, or planning to do something nice works to some extent.
- Actions: do something physical to get out of your head and into your body to create endorphins that make you feel good. In your car: sing out loud to uplifting songs.
- Results/body: notice if you are holding tension in your body and adopt a more relaxed posture.

Once the event is past, and we are feeling more relaxed, we can seek a more permanent solution by tackling the underlying belief on which the thought was based. Coaches call beliefs that we hold about ourselves, and that instigate a vicious cycle, 'limiting beliefs' because they limit what we believe is possible for us and act accordingly. Coaches call beliefs that we hold about ourselves, and that inspire a virtuous cycle, 'empowering beliefs' because they expand our capacity to experience positive emotions and achieve more. Whether you think you can't, or you can, it tends to become a self-fulfilling prophecy because of the cognitive behaviour cycle.

EXERCISE: REFRAME YOUR BELIEF FROM LIMITING TO EMPOWERING

Reframing means consciously arguing against, or reasoning with a limiting belief to see if something else (a more empowering belief) could be true. Write down your limiting belief then use one or more of these suggestions to unsettle the existing limiting belief and uncover a more empowering belief.

Trigger: I made a mistake in my work.

Limiting belief: *I am stupid.*

1. Counter example: what evidence do you have that the limiting belief is not always true? *I have a steady job, so I can't be entirely stupid.*

2. Establish causality: does having that limiting belief always lead to the unwanted outcome? *No, I don't always make mistakes.*

3. Fast-forward: what is the ultimate consequence of continuing to believe the limiting belief? What would you need to believe to get a different outcome? *If I believe I am stupid I will make more mistakes with my work and I'll end up without a job. If I believe that I only make mistakes when I rush, I can plan my time better and I'll keep my job.*

4. Generalise: is the limiting belief true for everyone? If not, what might they believe instead? *Not everyone is*

stupid and makes mistakes with their work; maybe they also believe they only make mistakes when they rush.

5. Reframe from an external viewpoint. *Sometimes we have a good laugh about the mistake; it's not all bad.*

6. Reframe from an internal viewpoint. *Even if I do something stupid, I'm human and everyone makes mistakes sometimes.*

Benefits for you

You will be able to notice and escape from a vicious cycle to avoid descending into a low mood, so you will stay positive and more resourceful. Over time you will put less strain on your body due to having to eliminate stress hormones. Empowering beliefs enable you to expand your capacity to achieve more.

Benefits for others

Others will feel more able to give you honest feedback and worry less about upsetting you because you are able to decide how to frame the feedback. For example, rather than thinking 'I am stupid' (vicious cycle) you will be able to reframe it as 'I did something stupid' (virtuous cycle).

Related habits

- Trigger: Prioritise your sphere of control (habit 1)
- Thoughts: Direct your focus (habit 2)

- Feelings: Process emotions as data (habit 15)
- Actions: Decide who is driving the bus (habit 11)
- Results: Be kind to yourself (habit 27)

Habit 17: Be Vulnerable and Surrender

This habit is about resolving an internal tension. Unlike habit 14, 'accept what is', which is about emotionally letting go of things outside your control, this habit is about emotionally letting go of pressure you are creating for yourself. The specific case of perfectionism is covered in habit 27, 'be kind to yourself'.

Vulnerability

Perhaps you're feeling emotionally vulnerable. That happens when we fall in love; we've given someone else the ability to hurt us emotionally, and we're trusting that they won't – at least, not intentionally. We can surrender and embrace the vulnerability as part of the process of emotional connectedness with someone else, or we can thrash ourselves by wanting both to fall in love and be certain that we won't be hurt. By definition, those things are mutually exclusive. It's biologically impossible to feel fear and love at the same time. It's easier in the long run to lean into the vulnerability and surrender to the emotion of love, while staying cognitively alert to behaviours that reinforce (or undermine) our belief that the other person is trustworthy. When we do this, we learn to trust our intuition or gut instinct to keep us safe, knowing that when we allow our feelings we are not weaker. We trust that our body is wired for survival and if there's cause to feel under threat then we'll be alert to the danger signals and can decide what to do next (see habit 15, 'process emotions as data'). Chapter six, 'Downtime', explains practices such as mindfulness that can help us tune into our instinct. In the workplace we can feel vulnerable when we share a confidence with someone, or when we are in our stretch zone and we are balancing growth and the increased likelihood of having our limitations exposed. Having a strong peer group (habit 7, 'design your peer group') can provide relationships where it feels safer to be vulnerable. Brené Brown articulates beautifully that courage and vulnerability are two sides of the same coin in her TED talk 'The Power of Vulnerability'.

Take the time and space to consider: What situations cause you to feel vulnerable? Are there any relationships that prompt you to feel vulnerable at the moment? Is there any action you need to take to address a niggle? What could be possible for you if you allowed more vulnerability?

> 'Vulnerability sounds like truth and feels like courage. Truth and courage aren't always comfortable, but they're never weakness.'
> – Brené Brown

Surrender

Let's look at an example. Despite your best resilience practices and good general health and fitness, you've become ill. It's inconvenient – it's always inconvenient for busy people!

If, at the first signs of being under the weather, you slow down and rest, your body can usually fight off the infection naturally in a day or so and you can get back to conquering the world. Learning to *listen to your body* was covered in the section on renewal in Resilience Fundamentals. If instead you dose up on over-the-counter flu remedy to mask the symptoms and soldier on, no doubt dragging yourself through the day underperforming and spreading germs to everyone else, it takes your body longer to heal. The net result is that you'd recover more quickly if you *surrendered* to the idea that you were becoming ill and let your body do its thing. An example of 'maximising value with minimal effort'. One of the side effects of not surrendering to the repair time your body is asking for is 'holiday sickness' when you've pushed to deliver high demands and then, when you finally take a holiday, you get sick.

Take a moment now to listen to your body and respond to what it needs, or at least schedule some time to address the need. Is there anything else you need to surrender to?

Benefits for you

You'll stop trying to fight battles (biology) you can't win. You'll feel less exhausted and save effort. You'll also recover far more quickly from illness. Being selectively vulnerable with others helps to build trust.

Benefits for others

Learning from your example, other people will feel they have permission not to be super-human, to invest in their own self-care and recognise that part of our strength comes from trusted relationships.

Related habits

- Design your peer group (habit 7)
- Manage your boundaries (habit 13) which includes asking for help
- Accept what is (habit 14)
- Process emotions as data (habit 15)
- Develop mindfulness (habit 19)
- Be kind to yourself (habit 27)

Habit 18: Work Through the Emotional Change Curve

Change is constant in life these days – both at work, with restructures and changing priorities, and at home, as our family cycles through the stages of life. It can be reassuring to be aware that when faced with change, there's a predictable emotional cycle that accompanies it. Acknowledging that you're human and you're susceptible to the same sequence of emotions can help you to moderate your emotional response and turn to established methods for moving through the sequence.

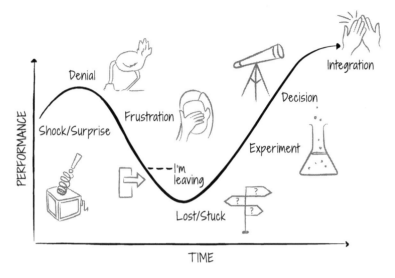

FIG. 5.2: EMOTIONAL CHANGE CURVE

The emotional change curve is based on the five stages of grief and loss described by Kubler-Ross and Kessler (2014): denial, anger, bargaining, depression and acceptance. The emotional change curve focuses on the loss of the status quo rather than the loss of a loved one, so it describes a more moderate emotional response and the language is more business-like.

The change curve shows the typical emotional journey for someone affected by a change. Some of us will move through the eight stages quickly, and others will take longer, depending on whether we naturally prefer to seek certainty or variety. We are sometimes on several emotional change curves at once, with changes happening at work (for example, a promotion or restructure) and at home (for example, moving house).

Because significant changes can challenge us mentally, emotionally, physically and spiritually this habit includes references to seventeen out of thirty of the resilience habits in the book, and it's one of the reasons I champion building your resilience proactively. A quieter time is not coming, change is a constant, so start now with whatever you have and select one habit that will support you in this moment – you can't learn them all at once.

These habits are useful at all stages of the change curve: habit 15, 'process emotions as data' so you notice the emotion, take appropriate action and let it pass. Habit 24, 'bite off what you can chew', influences the amount of pressure experienced and therefore the intensity of the emotions. If the demands are too high then these habits help to get it back under control: habit 12, 'maximise value with minimal effort', habit 13, 'manage your boundaries' and habit 26, 'speak your truth'. Habit 10, 'do energy accounting' to pace yourself. And if you're having a tough time with reconciling and important change use habit 25, 'know you always have four choices' to regain a sense of control.

EXAMPLE: CHANGE IN YOUR ORGANISATION

Stage of change curve	Response and additional useful habits
Shock/surprise	Your initial response to the change, which is usually short-lived. You have only just become aware of the change and you have little information other than knowing whether the change affects you. Habits to help you move forward: 'prioritise your sphere of control' (habit 1), 'accept what is' (habit 14).
Denial	You choose not to listen when it comes to change-related activities (for example, you conveniently have other work priorities that mean you don't go to change briefings). Your performance may increase as you 'dig in' to show that the old ways work just fine, or you may simply retreat to your comfort zone and hope the change will 'fizzle out'. Habits to help you move forward: 'accept what is' (habit 14), 'know you always have four choices' (habit 25).
Frustration	You are informing others of, or being advised of, the new ways of working and trying to go along with it, but the process is not yet smooth and you're doing things more slowly because the new processes are unfamiliar. Meanwhile, the 'business as usual' demands are still pressing. Stay with it – the new ways of working will get easier. Habits to help you move forward: 'develop a growth mindset' (habit 28), 'create your happy file' (habit 23).
I'm leaving	You feel disillusioned with the future vision, you no longer feel aligned with the company's purpose or culture, or you can already see that you are no longer a good skills-fit for future opportunities. Clearly not everyone working through the emotional change curve will choose to leave, but many will consider it and actively choose to stay. Habits to help you move forward: 'achieve personal alignment' (habit 8), 'accept what is' (habit 14).

Stage of change curve	Response and additional useful habits
Lost/stuck	You are not sure that you see yourself in the future vision, but you don't want to leave. You've tried the new ways, but they take you a long time and feel clunky. It all feels a bit overwhelming and you're not sure what to do to get back in control of your workload and do what's now being asked of you. It's an emotional low point. Habits to help you move forward: 'be kind to yourself' (habit 27), 'avoid vicious cycles' (habit 16). What else you can do: identify and make progress on small, well-defined steps so you can feel you're winning at something and get your mojo back. Then 'decide who is driving the bus' (habit 11).
Experiment	You're feeling more informed and reinvigorated, with the expectation that the worst is now behind you. The way forward is becoming clearer as more information comes to light and you see others embracing the change. You're 'giving it a go' by working in the new ways, and you feel less discouraged than you did if things don't go entirely to plan. You are cautiously optimistic about the future, but your mood can still go either way: it depends on how each day goes and what results you get. Habits to help you move forward: 'develop a growth mindset' (habit 28), 'be kind to yourself' (habit 27).
Decision	You've had enough successes with the new ways of working to feel convinced that the changes are here to stay. You now feel personally aligned with the future and optimistic about what is coming next. You're a positive role model for those still getting to grips with the new ways of working. Habits to help you move forward: 'use role models and mentors' (habit 6).

Stage of change curve	Response and additional useful habits
Integration	The 'new way' is now 'the way': you're proficient at it and feeling competent and confident again after a period of adjustment. You can role-model the new ways and have a well-earned respite while the rest of the organisation catches up.
	Habits to help you move forward: 'create your happy file' (habit 23) and 'develop mindfulness' (habit 19) to maximise learning and insight from the change journey.

EXERCISE: REFLECT ON A CHANGE YOU ARE EXPERIENCING

1. Think of a current change that is impacting you
2. Reflect on where you are on the emotional change curve
3. Use the table to help you decide what action you can take to move yourself forward
4. Take action

Alternatively, get your team, or family, together and discuss where each person is on the curve and how you can best support each other to collectively move forward.

The emotional change curve is not a one-way ticket: it is possible to move back and forth between some of the stages before gaining momentum. That's OK, as long as you're moving further forward overall.

Benefits for you

By normalising an emotional sequence, it feels more predictable and acceptable. You'll be able to recognise that it will pass in the fullness of time.

Benefits for others

Having a shared language and diagram for discussing emotions during a change programme can inform discussions about how best to support one another.

Related habits

- Focus (habit 1)
- Role models (habits 6, 8)
- Energy (habits 10, 11, 12, 13)
- Emotions (habits 14, 15, 16)
- Downtime (habit 19)
- Optimism (habits 23, 24, 25, 26)
- Meaning (habits 27, 28)

CHAPTER SIX

Downtime

Typically, our downtime is a period of sleep, rest or meditation. Sleep was covered in chapter four on 'Energy'. Playfulness and laughter are also great ways to relax. We have learned that the sympathetic nervous system creates a chemical response that prepares us for 'fight, flight or freeze'. The parasympathetic nervous system does the opposite; it reduces our state of alertness once the perceived threat has passed. It's often called the 'rest and digest' response. This is our downtime.

When we are feeling under pressure, our ability to enjoy life is often one of the first casualties, as we forgo fun to knuckle down and get the work done. But all work and no play will make anyone miserable, and it soon starts to feel like a life half lived. We begin to wonder whether sacrificing our happiness is worth it, and we find ourselves on a slippery slope to the vicious cycle we covered earlier (see habit 16, 'avoid vicious cycles'). What do you do that is joyful and makes you laugh?

TOP TIPS: BUILDING MORE DOWNTIME INTO YOUR DIARY

- Take at least twenty minutes for lunch every day.
- Book holidays in advance: gain more benefit by anticipating a welcome break.
- Schedule your time so that each week includes a mix of activities that are routine (sleep, eat), necessary (work, food shopping) and pleasurable (hobbies, meet friends).
- Laugh! Allow yourself to be silly, see the world through the eyes of a child, or watch a comedy sketch.
- Protect your downtime fiercely so you don't end up using time you set aside to accommodate work that has overrun or unexpected demands on your time.

Why it matters

Incorporating guilt-free downtime is important to our body, mind, emotions and spirit.

Body: When we put fewer demands on our body it can go into repair mode, keeping us healthy and allowing us to return with renewed energy. Did you know that if you have been awake for seventeen hours or more your reduced alertness and response time is equivalent of being over the alcohol limit for driving? When we have downtime, our bodies have a chance to eliminate the 'fight, flight or freeze' hormones generated by a stress response. Light yoga or gentle walks count as downtime, but a hard session at the gym doesn't. While that is time away from work and has many other health benefits, it's part of your foundational work, not what we're covering here as downtime.

Mind: When we have relaxed attention, we provide space for our subconscious to make connections between things we know, giving us further insight. After learning something new, having a good night's sleep is like hitting the 'save' button. We also feel more resourceful, think more clearly and have a more grounded presence.

Emotions: When we pause and reflect, we often take ourselves away from the thing that is triggering stress and are able to gain more perspective, which allows us to moderate our emotional response to events. Getting enough rest and sleep is important for regulating our mood. When you regularly take time to be more light-hearted, you are more able to look on the bright side and be resourceful when things don't go to plan.

Spirit: What does it mean to you to have a life that is fully lived? Allow yourself to get off the hamster wheel of striving and doing – you're a human being, not a human doing. Periods of rest allow us to enjoy pursuits that express all of who we are, enjoy nature, daydream, experience wonder at the incredible beauty in all people and all things, and be grateful for our blessings. When we are light-hearted, we are more fun to be around. Rest allows us to pay relaxed attention to things we'd like to do that would allow us to feel that when we die, we have lived a full life experience and made magical memories with those we care about. Don't save everything for retirement: you might not get there, or you might not have the means or health to do it. Live life as you go.

This chapter includes habits for renewing your energy, making meaningful connections with people and being more light-hearted.

19. Develop mindfulness – learn to calm your mind to enjoy the present moment, gain perspective, refresh your concentration or sleep soundly.

20. Minimise digital distractions – partially or fully disconnecting from our devices can help us to focus, find calm and connect with others.

21. Express your true spirit – rediscovering what makes you feel *you* and showing up as your *whole* self, wherever you are.

22. Create magic moments – doing nice things for others and enjoying the sense of connection and joy.

Habit 19: Develop Mindfulness

Mindfulness is a therapeutic technique to achieve a mental state of awareness on the present moment, while calmly noticing and accepting any thoughts, feelings and physical sensations. If you struggle to switch off at the end of the day, or wake up with your to-do list already running, it's worth finding a handful of solutions that enable you to experience mental calm to give your brain a 'cognitive break' so that you lessen production of stress hormones and are able to return with fresh attention for the next task.

It's worth noting that this habit is one that should be done on its own so you can be fully present in the moment, not in combination with other habits as advocated in habit 12 ('maximise value with minimal effort'). To illustrate, a gentle stroll noticing nature, the breeze and letting thoughts float through your mind is mindful, a power walk while listening to a personal development audio book and searching for insights is not mindful, it's effortful.

I'll admit that developing mindfulness was one of the habits I found hardest of all in the beginning. I tried yoga, spa days, massages, mindfulness recordings, meditation practice, long baths, colouring books for adults... in desperation I even spent three days on a silent retreat at a Buddhist monastery (the first time I went it was hell!). At times, the process did not seem relaxing at all, but I'm glad I stayed with it.

Meditation

I learned that sitting absolutely still and silent and focusing on my breathing doesn't always work for me; I find 'active meditation' is much easier. Active meditation is light repetitive work that doesn't tax the brain or body but provides focus and rhythm. Examples include weeding, gentle walks, painting the garden fence... you get the idea. If you're new to meditation, I recommend an app called Headspace. (www .headspace.com). The app has ten free meditations to help you to get started with the practice of allowing thoughts to float through your mind without getting attached to them.

Cognitive breaks

A long span of intellectual endeavour without breaks results in declining performance. Achieving a state of mental calm provides a 'cognitive break' to refresh our capacity to think effectively, yet too many people still try to maintain an intense focus for the entire working day, even eating lunch at their desks. During training, even after explaining the benefits of having a cognitive break to 'reboot' our attention and 'save' everything we've done, I notice that some workshop delegates still spend the break checking their email, and ultimately reducing their return on investment for the training! To work smarter not harder, we need to consciously break our conditioning and realise the value of taking breaks.

When you take cognitive breaks, you will notice the benefits quickly. I get it: if all your colleagues are eating lunch at their desk, you might be concerned that they'll think you're slacking off if you go for a twenty-minute lunch break in the fresh air. If you do it deliberately and explain why, you'll soon start to influence their behaviour; they'll also take a break, and everyone will be more productive in the afternoon because of it. If they don't change their habits, act in the best interests of your health, sanity and productivity anyway! Even a walk to the vending machine and back provides a cognitive break, as long as you are not thinking about work as you walk!

Mind-full-ness

It is also possible to achieve a state of mindfulness (or flow) when you do an activity you find pleasurable that requires 100% concentration on the task at hand – I can achieve that through coaching or dancing; my dad rides his motorbike. Although you are 100% mentally engaged in the activity, you are still having a break from stress-inducing hormones. Experiment and find out what works for you.

Write it down

If you have a busy head, writing the thought down can allow your mind to let go of the thought: once it's on paper you can't forget it and your brain won't need to keep giving you regular reminders. I found this useful while I was writing my PhD thesis. I often woke in the middle of the night with a bright idea, so I left a pad and pen on my bedside table. When I woke up, I could jot down a note and go back to sleep.

Ring-fence your worries

Worries can make it harder to calm your mind. To ring-fence your worries and free your mind to focus on other things, try this exercise:

EXERCISE: SCHEDULE WORRY TIME

1. Schedule a specific time for worrying by putting a 'worry hour' in your diary.

2. When a worrying thought arises, add it to the notes in the worry hour, let it go and return to what you were doing. Your brain knows now that you won't forget to worry, so it stops reminding you all the time.

3. By the time you get to the scheduled worry time, you'll have slept on some of the items and they'll no longer seem relevant. If there's anything left, you've got a set time to worry about it.

4. When worry hour is over, note down any ongoing worries for your next scheduled worry time. Then get on with something else to distract you – your worry time is up.

Benefits for you

Mindfulness is a key habit in stress reduction and improving overall happiness. By increasing your appreciation of the present moment, you are less likely to get caught up in worries about the future or regrets over the past. Creating mental space from the demands of the day provides the opportunity to gain a larger perspective on life. Mindfulness can also help relieve stress, treat heart disease, lower blood pressure, reduce chronic pain and improve sleep.

Benefits for others

When you are able to calm your mind, others will be able to sense that you are more present and attentive during discussions leading to improved relationships and heightened connection.

Related habits

- Direct your focus (habit 2)
- Make a decision (habit 4)
- Manage your boundaries (habit 13)
- Accept what is (habit 14)
- Avoid vicious cycles (habit 16)
- Minimise digital distractions (habit 20)

Habit 20: Minimise Digital Distractions

Technology is amazing: it places in our palm the world of digitised information and the ability to connect with people anywhere with just a swipe or a tap of a finger. It can also cause you to become a distraction junkie, hooked on the dopamine hit of social approval. It can also give you a cortisol hit of stress when you have a fear of missing out or you read or contribute to a heated debate on a complex subject reduced to short soundbites. With all the notifications, pings, alerts and vibrations, it's hard to focus your attention on one thing. Even if your phone is switched off, having it within eyesight is still distracting because you're conditioned to it being on. It also signals to whoever you're with that you're not giving them your full attention. Put your devices out of sight to increase focus, rapport and connection.

If you work in emergency services or you're 'on call', of course you need to be contactable – by a subset of people, during your contracted hours. If you're a parent, you may be reassured to know that you can be contacted day or night if your children need you. There are technology settings that make that possible. For example, adding your nearest and dearest to your list of favourites on your contacts lets you shut most of the world out but stay accessible to a few.

Technology is fantastic when it works for *us*, not the other way around. It's a tool for a job, and many people would benefit from having more boundaries (see habit 13, 'Manage your boundaries') and self-control around their digital world. The best bit about technology is that it comes with an 'off' switch – or you can at least suppress the notifications. Switch to 'pull' instead of 'push' mode for email refresh, switch to aeroplane mode, or use 'do not disturb' at night to reduce incoming distractions. There is a good deal of satisfaction in deliberately having more control over your devices and the time you spend on them.

Since January 2017 the French Labour Code has included the 'right to disconnect', which means that if an employee is not contactable on their mobile phone outside of working hours it cannot be considered as misconduct. The law reflects that digital technologies have blurred the line between work and private lives and that the right to disconnect is necessary for the mental and emotional health of employees.

One way to regain control (or at least see how addicted you are!) is to have a full digital detox. That means switching off all technology devices for a period of time. No TV, no Internet, no Alexa, no radio, no phone, no devices and no smart watch. Digital detox is about allowing ourselves mental calming. Or as I call it – unplugging to recharge. I have a full digital detox week every year just to prove to myself I can still do it! My preferred hideaway is a cottage in the countryside with no Wi-Fi or phone signal. That makes abstinence easier, as it requires less willpower, but it achieves the same result. I return home feeling like I had three weeks off, not one.

When we have a large project to work on, such as detailed analysis or writing a report, a more moderate digital detox can significantly increase our productivity levels. For example, turning off your email and phone so you can focus on just one thing at a time. If you need to, quickly check both email and phone for any urgent messages around midday, then return to focused work.

TOP TIPS: DAILY DIGITAL DETOX

- Many firms in France support a digital detox by switching off their email servers from 7pm to 7am so workers can't send emails out of hours. Give yourself a twelve-hour break from digital distractions (eg iPhone has a 'do not disturb' function).

- Have a two-hour period every day where you switch off all digital distractions and focus on a single task that requires your full concentration.

- Have a separate phone for work. It helps give you control over how accessible you are to colleagues – for example, evenings, weekends and when you're on holiday.
- Have a one-day digital detox every weekend to maximise connection with family and friends and regain a sense of control over your technology.
- When driving, put your mobile phone in the glovebox.

Remember, digital detox is about working smarter, not harder. There is no such thing as multitasking, just high overheads of mentally switching between tasks. If our attention is distracted, we are less focused and less productive, and we take longer to get the same work done.

Benefits for you

Many of the demands on you are perceived, not real, 'on call' demands. Does it really matter if you go for two hours without checking your email? Digital detox makes it easier to be mindful. By practising your patience muscle (no instant gratification, no Google!) you will re-assert your self-control and become immune to advertising, enticements and chemical hits from screen-induced stimulation. You'll be more able to rest and digest.

Benefits for others

Others won't feel obliged to respond to out-of-hours emails if you aren't sending them. They'll be able to communicate with you more clearly and with less room for misunderstanding, if you have a conversation during work hours rather than by email. You'll be more present, and others will feel more valued, if your phone is out of sight during time together.

Related habits

- Direct your focus (habit 2)
- Maximise value with minimal effort (habit 12)
- Manage your boundaries (habit 13)
- Develop mindfulness (habit 19)
- Express your true spirit (habit 21)

Habit 21: Express Your True Spirit

Spirit is the essence of what makes you *you*; and it's wonderfully different for each of us. Children show their spirit all the time: they haven't yet learned social conditioning, and they exhibit a freedom of expression and creativity that we can enjoy as adults only if we allow ourselves. It is effortless, because it's who we are when we are not hindered by societal expectations. It's the quiet inner voice of self-acceptance that says, 'this is me, and all is well'. It is the encouragement of our higher self that believes we are truly magnificent and resourceful, capable of so much more than we realise.

You know you're living a spirited life when:

- You have an inner peace based on self-acceptance
- You don't feel the need to fit in and don't care to be accepted
- You feel optimistic
- You live in the moment and embrace all that life has to offer
- You experience joy and laughter regularly
- Work and play feel in flow, and life is good
- You don't hang around where you are not wanted and valued
- You are not judgemental: you accept others are living life by their rules

Some of the things that get in the way of us being more spirited are:

- Low physical energy
- Being disconnected from ourselves
- Feeling overwhelmed or inadequate
- Playing small so others don't feel threatened
- Believing that life is supposed to be a struggle, that there's no gain without pain

EXERCISE: CONNECT WITH YOUR SPIRIT

Choosing to live a life that feels fully lived can be easier and more fun than you imagine. First ensure you are well rested and relaxed, then try some, or all, of these ideas to tune in to your feelings, intuition and gut instinct and learn to trust yourself. The journey to self-love and self-acceptance can take time, but the prize is spiritual freedom.

Recall a time when you were less self-conscious. Think back, what did you love to do as a child? Is there any version of that in your life now, or could there be? What part of your spirit would you like to express more often? Could you satisfy the need through a hobby?

For example, as a child I wanted to be an actor like my big brother. Now I deliver training (a bit like being on stage) and invite delegates to change the way they look at the world and interact with it by discussing different skills, insights and perspectives.

I also used to enjoy dancing lessons as a child. I started dancing lessons again in my mid-forties and absolutely love the creativity of freestyle musical expression with a dance partner. When I'm dancing, I feel wonderfully feminine and experience flow – hours pass in minutes.

Suspend judgement. There is no 'right way' when it comes to spirit; you are uniquely and wonderfully you. Do it your way, whatever that is. What would you do if time, energy and resources were not an issue? What would you do if you did not need approval from others? What would you do if you knew you could not fail? What is an achievable first step to living a life that is more *you*?

Life imitating art. Which film characters have a spirit that resonates with you? What songs feel as though they were written for you? Music can empower the listener just as much as it does the artist. There are lots of songs with empowering themes that call us to express all of who we are. You'll have your own preferences for era and genre. Try searching for empowering playlists online, and choose the songs that remind you it's great to be you. Hopefully, they'll help inspire you to live your life as loudly and authentically as you choose.

Here are some ways people attending my workshops have told me they express their spirit, either alone or with others:

TOP TIPS: EXPRESSING YOUR SPIRIT

- **Play**: be playful or silly.
- **Compete**: at sport or work out.
- **Connect**: enjoy camaraderie at football. Build communities. Have amazing sex.
- **Campaign** on topics that are meaningful for you.
- **Nurture**: take care of children. Be of service to others.
- **Explore**: travel. Walk in natural landscapes. Get lost on purpose.
- **Create**: invent gadgets. Dance. Sing. Make art.

What are you doing when you experience flow, when you lose all track of time? If you're in flow, that's a good indication that you've found your thing!

Let your colours show. Expressing your true spirit means expressing all of who you are and not holding anything back or hiding. Often, it's easier to do this outside work at first – but ideally, be true to who you are at work as well (in a way that fits the context and is culturally sensitive). Showing others all of who you are is an expression of self-confidence and self-acceptance. It can take some courage if you're breaking the norm of your peer group, but it's well worth the risk – test the water first until you get comfortable with it. If you're a geek, gay, religious, a hippy or a fashionista, let your colours show. You are not a robot – embrace who you are, even if that small expression means wearing crazy socks or a statement piece of jewellery with a run-of-the-mill suit. Find a way to be you on a daily basis.

You have everything inside of you that you need, so let it out.

Benefits for you

When you express your true spirit, you'll feel comfortable in your own skin, fully alive, delighting in who you are as a person and not needing external validation for how you show up in the world. When you feel spirited, you are more likely to try new things and go beyond your comfort zone. Emotions are contagious, and the energy created by expressing our true spirit draws others to us: friends, lovers, business partners.

Benefits for others

Seeing a range of different personalities indirectly gives others permission to be themselves too. A self-assured but humble expression of self gives others confidence that you are grounded and will not easily be swayed by public opinion or adverse events. You're also likely to be light-hearted and much more fun to be around.

Related habits

- Decide who is driving the bus (habit 11)
- Accept what is (habit 14)
- Be vulnerable and surrender (habit 17)
- Speak your truth (habit 26)

Habit 22: Create Magic Moments

We all need love and connection. Spending time with people who make us smile, lift our spirits, tell good jokes and are easy to talk to is a great way to meet that need in a positive way.

Magic moments

Our spirit is nurtured in those magic moments that make us feel truly alive: moments we want to savour and commit to memory. We can create magic moments for ourselves or others; all it takes is some thought about what might constitute a magic moment and a little imagination to make it happen. A magic moment doesn't have to be big or expensive: most people just want our time and our undivided attention.

Usually we consider what the other person might enjoy and then hope they like it, but there's a way to increase our success rate! There are five *love* languages (Chapman, 2015) that explain the different ways we recognise when someone has expressed love towards us. That 'someone' doesn't have to be a romantic partner; it can be anyone we want to show *appreciation* to, including colleagues (Chapman and White, 2010). Here are examples of five ways to show love or appreciation to partners, and to work colleagues.

1. Telling them, for example, sharing a passage, poem or song that expresses your appreciation; offering targeted praise to an individual at work.

2. Spending time together doing something you both enjoy, or gifting them some quality 'me time' by taking the children out for the day; going for lunch with a colleague and not discussing work.

3. Doing something to make their day easier or more enjoyable, such as cooking dinner or arranging a surprise picnic on a sunny day; supporting someone with a task, or shielding them from interruptions so they can concentrate.

4. Giving them something, like surprise tickets to an event you know they want to attend; registering a colleague for a conference or special event.

5. Making a physical connection; for example, offering a neck and shoulder rub after a long day; a firm handshake or high five in the workplace.

We tend to seek connection with others in the same way that we like to receive it, unless we know the other person's preference. If you want to know what someone else's preference is but you don't want to ask, watch what they do for others. When we create magic moments for someone else, and the moment we create is aligned with the other person's preference, it significantly increases the effect of the magic because they feel that you understand and care for them.

EXERCISE: CREATE MAGIC MOMENTS

1. Complete this quiz www.5lovelanguages.com/profile to discover *your* top love language (and to get more examples)

2. Guess, or ask, the preferred love language of the person/people you want to create a magic moment for

3. Think about what they might like that you can achieve within time and budget

4. Plan the details and keep it a surprise until you are sure you can deliver it

5. Watch their face light up as you tell them, or they experience the magic moment

**CASE STUDY: BALANCING WORK
AND HOME COMMITMENTS**

I'm the financial director of a sizeable charity. The combination of being passionate about our purpose, having a small team and my professional pride meant that I worked long hours all year. I had planned to work at home over the Christmas break too, until my coaching session and re-evaluating my priorities. The resilience habits in this book have stopped my busy head so I can be an effective financial director at work AND an amazing mum at home... now I'm creating magic memories with my boys that will last a lifetime instead of observing them from behind a laptop/mobile... priceless. I have proven to myself that when I return to work fully rested, I blast through the work in a fraction of the time, so everyone wins.

– Karan Johal, Financial Director

Spontaneous smiles

A smaller version of magic moments is spontaneous smiles. We can create and enjoy these every day if we choose, even with strangers. No one complains at random acts of kindness. Give others something to smile about and you'll feel good too. Here are some examples:

1. Send a short text so they know you are thinking about them

2. Ask 'how are you' and be fully present to hear their answer

3. Hold the door open for someone or let a car out in front of you

4. Offer the newspaper you just finished to another commuter

5. Initiate a 'high five' or 'fist bump' with someone you know well

Benefits for you

When you are planning a magic moment for someone else you get to pre-enjoy the event as you anticipate their joy. Whether you are part of the magic moment, or hear about it afterwards, you can enjoy the improved relationship with the other person created by better communication and increased understanding. Laughter releases happy hormones that offset stress hormones. Life is short, so enjoy it!

Benefits for others

When you do nice things, it creates magic moments for others, and they feel more connected to you. Smiles are contagious, so when you smile you make others happier too. When other people feel uplifted, they are more likely to be kind towards the next person they meet, and experience for themselves the joy of creating a spontaneous smile. Happier humans, better world.

Related habits

- Create your happy file (habit 23)
- Give back (habit 30)

CHAPTER SEVEN

Optimism

Southwick and Charney (2012) define optimism as 'a future-oriented attitude, involving hope and confidence that things will turn out well'. Cultivating an optimistic outlook is the golden rule in resilience. If we don't believe that a positive outcome is possible, we will not invest in the other areas of personal resilience: what would be the point? If you don't currently default to optimism in at least some areas of your life, this is the place to start. Optimism and pessimism are both contagious. The good news is that we can learn to be optimistic even if we didn't have optimistic role models during our early years.

A ten-question assessment of whether you are more optimistic or pessimistic can be found here www.psytoolkit.org /survey-library/optimism-lotr.html.

Sometimes in life we experience adversity: events that are outside our control and that we would not have chosen.

Illness, an accident, a bereavement, being a victim of crime, or redundancy are just a few. Optimism is often misunderstood to be a belief that 'everything will be all right'. Well, 'everything' is not within our control (see habit 1, 'prioritise your sphere of control'), so how can we possibly know that everything will be all right? Optimism is more accurately described as the belief that 'whatever happens, I will be all right'. If you are optimistic about your ability to respond to an adverse event then the statement is more believable, because your response to the event is within your control. If you have a record of pulling through adverse life events, you'll have learned a thing or two about how to navigate new ones. Then the statement 'whatever happens, I will be all right' is easier to believe, for you and for others.

Optimism doesn't mean ignoring the hard or challenging things in life, but it does mean changing how you approach them. An optimist believes that in general things will go well, and any adverse events are inconveniences to be navigated before things start to go well again. A healthy dose of cynicism can help to ensure our thinking is robust – *if* the cynic within us is willing to let go of expectations about the outcome. A pessimist believes that in general things will go wrong and any periods of ease or good fortune are likely to be short-lived before things return to going wrong again. A superbly descriptive term for a pessimist is 'mood hoover', because a pessimist seems to suck all the energy out of a room.

TOP TIP: PRACTISING GRATITUDE

Noticing the blessings you have, regardless of your situation, puts you in a more positive mood. It dampens your cortisol (stress) levels and supports your resilience because you shift your focus (habit 2, 'direct your focus') to all that's right with the world, rather than focusing on what is not as you'd like it to be.

Writing down three things to be grateful for before you go to sleep can give you a more restful night. It doesn't matter if you repeat the same thing on different days but try to see how many different things you can be grateful for.

Why it matters

Optimism is important because it reduces our physiological arousal, which means that our brains can maintain a breadth of focus, thoughts and behaviours. Thinking broadly enables us to be creative, inclusive and flexible in our thoughts, helping us find solutions that will help us through an adverse event. If others believe you are capable of realistic optimism during times of change and ambiguity, they will have a greater sense of certainty.

The habits in this chapter support the sense that 'whatever happens, I will be alright'.

23. Create your happy file – reflecting on past experience and magic moments to create a resource that reminds you that you are already capable and resilient.

24. Bite off what you can chew – breaking tasks into manageable chunks and getting the pace of change right so you move consistently in the direction of your dreams.

25. Know you always have four choices – a sense that you are self-directed in all situations supports your confidence.

26. Speak your truth – knowing you have a voice and can make yourself heard strengthens your courage and gives you confidence that if you need help you can request it.

Habit 23: Create Your 'Happy File'

Congratulations, you've survived life so far! No doubt there have been obstacles and challenges that you have navigated, and you are probably more resourceful, creative and capable than you think. In moments of self-doubt (we all have them), it can lift your spirits to recall times when you have succeeded at life and to remember the lessons you have already learned from adversity.

EXERCISE: START YOUR HAPPY FILE

In an electronic or a box file, gather together positive feedback and testimonials you have received over the years. Once you've started your happy file, you can add to it as you continue succeeding.

Think right back: it doesn't matter if you're now a CEO and you put your childhood cycling proficiency certificate in your happy file. If going out on your bike on a main road felt like a stretch at the time and it feels good to remember that triumph, then include it. Suspend judgement and include anything that made – or makes – you feel loved, capable and positive about life. No one else is going to see it anyway.

Here are a few things my clients have told me they include:

- Photos of happy times
- Keepsakes
- Old letters and cards from special people or with heartfelt messages
- Client testimonials or references
- Certificates and awards
- Old passports with lots of stamps from different countries

EXERCISE: ADD YOUR VISION BOARD

After you've compiled your happy file, or when you've just reviewed the contents and you're feeling especially capable, it's a great time to look ahead and imagine what you'd like to include in your happy file in the next year or so. I'm an executive coach: you didn't think I'd write an entire book without mentioning a vision board, did you? The reason vision boards have remained so appealing over time is because they work. Having a vision of the future we want to create gives us a reason to gather our courage and commit ourselves to achieving more than we are currently capable of. The act of creating a vision demonstrates our optimism about the future. It also helps us to focus on a few things rather than many (see habit 2, 'direct your focus'). That focus increases the likelihood that we'll notice people, events and opportunities that will move us towards achieving our desires.

- Add to your happy file one to four images that represent what you want to be, do or have within the next year.

We have all failed at work in some capacity, whether it was a deadline that slipped, a clunky conversation or not delivering the expected results. We have all failed in life too: birthdays forgotten, hearts broken, actions we now regret. Sometimes it was our actions that were lacking, and sometimes an unpredictable event changed the landscape. Often it was a little of both. When life doesn't go to plan, we often say we get 'experience' and that it's 'character building', and it is – if we *learn* from the experience. Messing up can also be career-limiting or even career-ending, and that's when it's even more helpful to get the most learning and value from the experience. Doing so ensures that we don't repeat our mistakes, and nor does anyone else, and we limit reputational damage by owning our mistakes and learning from them.

EXERCISE: ADD YOUR LESSONS LEARNED

Think about the lessons you have learned from adversity. While we might not have chosen the adversity and we don't want to dwell there, the fact that we emerged on the other side means that we are survivors. It is also highly likely that there are positives you can take from that experience, which have shaped the person you are today.

Remember, optimism isn't some fairy-tale view of a world full of unicorns: it's grounded in reality. That's what makes it believable to you and others. So, take a deep breath and set some time aside to dive back into the murky past and see what wisdom it has for you. This is not a pity party; think of it as an archaeological dig with clear outcomes.

Recall up to twelve adverse experiences and create an index card for each, eg car crash, divorce, failed project, made redundant. You might want to review them to discover your core values (see habit 8, 'achieve personal alignment'). Or, if you already know them, you could simply write your core values on some index cards – in many ways, knowing what an adverse event told you about your values was the lesson from that event. Is there anything else from that adversity that you want to take forward as a lesson into your future?

- For each adversity card: briefly write the lesson learned (and possibly a core value), then add the card to your happy file.

Mix up all the happy memories, lessons learned and vision images in your happy file. When you next look through it, you'll come across some of each – it will help you stay in a good place emotionally while taking lessons from the past into the future.

If you are experiencing a low mood or want to gather your courage before a big event, look through your happy file to remind yourself of the good times, and of how capable and resilient you are.

Benefits for you

Committing to add to your happy file reminds you to celebrate your wins so that you pause occasionally and don't get caught in the trap of constantly striving, which is exhausting. Looking through your happy file reminds you of the lessons you learned in hard times that have made you stronger and the person you are today. It reassures you that you are a resourceful human being, capable of navigating whatever life throws at you, and reminds you to take action towards your vision.

Benefits for others

Creating your happy file is largely a private activity, but you could tell others (especially young children) about the technique so that they can create their own. If you share your lessons learned with others, it offers them wisdom and perspective and makes it acceptable for them to take risks and learn from their mistakes.

Related habits

- Direct your focus (habit 2)
- Decide who is driving the bus (habit 11)
- Be kind to yourself (habit 27)

Habit 24: Bite Off What You Can Chew

Years of experience in change management and in coaching talented professionals have shown me that high performers, as a cohort, are spectacularly good at shooting themselves in the foot by taking on too much. This habit will help you avoid doing that. Highly talented and highly capable people are often also highly ambitious, and that's great! This habit is not about playing small; quite the opposite. If you have a courageous goal then breaking it down helps you to maintain focus, better estimate the effort required, maintain steady progress and collaborate with others who can help you achieve it. On the other hand, don't buy in to repeated stretch if it's not what you need right now. To attain and then sustain high performance, there's an art and a science to biting off what you can chew. Change managers call this getting the pace of change right.

> **INCONVENIENT TRUTH**
> You are human.

This habit is based on the change formula popularised by Dannemiller and Jacobs (1992). It helps us to assess the size of the task before we begin, and to prime our motivation to start. Don't be alarmed – it's fake maths, and a description follows.

$$C = (D \times V \times F) > R$$

C = **Change**

D = **Dissatisfaction** with current state

V = **Vision** of what is possible

F = **First steps** that can be taken towards the vision

R = **Resistance**

FIG. 7.1: THE CHANGE FORMULA

The change formula expresses the idea that to generate momentum and change, we need to have a gap between our dissatisfaction with how things are now (D) and our vision of how they could be in future (V). We also need to have an idea of reasonable first steps we could take to close the gap (F). These three things, when taken together, have to outweigh the resistance we feel towards getting started (R). If the resistance feels too great, you're in the panic zone and biting off more than you can chew. Revise your goal by reviewing the elements D, V and F until the goal feels like a stretch, but an achievable one if you are 'realistically optimistic'. If you need a better idea of how to estimate the gap, ask around, do research or do a pilot first. It's important to note that, like maths, if any of D, V or F are missing (zero), then the whole bracket is zero and no change is possible because resistance is always greater than zero. All elements must be present to some degree. Here's a worked example:

EXAMPLE: USING THE CHANGE FORMULA
TO SET STRETCH GOALS

First pass:

D	My career has stalled, and I'm ready for more.
V	I have been offered the opportunity to 'act up' into a promotion role effective as of next week.
F	Clear my social diary, I foresee working long hours for the next month at least.
	Get a few friends lined up to help with the house move.
	Brief my existing team that I'm not going to be as available to them, and I'll only be able to cover escalated risks and issues. We'll all have to 'suck it up' for a short while.
	Say yes to the full remit of the new role. I have been waiting for this opportunity, and I'm not going to look weak now.
R	I know I want the next role up, but the level of responsibility and visibility is daunting. I need to hit the ground running as the person doing the role left suddenly, and I will end up bridging both roles for a while. My existing team is already under-resourced due to current financial pressures. I'm about to move to a new house too.
Result	Panic zone: hesitation creates doubt for self and others.

Second pass:

D	My career has stalled, and I'm ready for more.
V	I have been offered the opportunity to 'act up' into a promotion role effective as of next week.
F	Delegate or delay whatever I can to provide others opportunity to step up and to move non-critical activity to a later date. If necessary, take the budget hit and get someone else to support the team temporarily.
	See who else can do the big speaking event next Friday, or get some top-quality mentoring, fast!
	Upgrade our removal service, I'm not going to have time to pack boxes, and I don't want the additional effort to fall to my partner. Any decluttering will have to happen after the move.
R	It's a stretch for sure, but it's do-able if I stay focused on high-value activity, act in the best interests of the company and continue to practice my resilience habits. It's time to ramp up my self-care.
Result	Wow, I've been waiting for this opportunity. This is my time to shine.

'Dissatisfaction' doesn't just mean moving away from something you don't want, it could also mean you're not currently well positioned to say 'yes' to a rare opportunity to do something you do want (for example, if you received a surprise invite to a skiing trip with friends, would you be fit enough to enjoy it?). Be completely honest with yourself about where you are today. Don't give the slightly polished version of the truth you'd tell at an interview. See your current situation as it is – no better, no worse and no judgement.

CASE STUDY: BREAKING DOWN BIG GOALS TO CREATE A SUSTAINABLE PACE

I'm a very ambitious first-time managing director, looking to make my mark by disrupting the legal services industry. I'm a fast-paced person, so my tendency is to want results within days, not years. As a business owner – particularly for a start up, you do work crazy hours and put everything into your venture to make it a success. As I'm determined and have a very strong sense of purpose, I have always been happy to put the hours in and make my vision a reality, but I realised that I needed to re-assess my daily habits to make sure my performance is sustainable, and I can actually turn my vision into a reality. By breaking the big goals down into quarterly and monthly targets I can be confident of delivery and enjoy a sense of progress. I also set myself daily goals and make sure I incorporate my daily resilience habits into my routine which means that whatever challenge we face, I am physically and mentally prepared to take it on.

– Carrie Caladine, Owner and Managing Director, Right Legal Group

Once you have established a stretch goal, acknowledge any resistance that shows up and make a start as soon as you know the first few steps. You can figure out the rest as you go along. Do what you can today and do a bit more tomorrow. If you are off the pace for a day then get back to it as soon as you can, and you'll move ever closer towards your goal.

Benefits for you

By actively managing the demands on you, and making steady progress towards realistic stretch goals, you will restore your faith in your ability to change outcomes and be able to move forward with confidence and optimism. You will build a reputation based on consistently delivering outside your comfort zone and still have spare capacity to enjoy time away from work or be able to step up to short sprints of heroic effort.

Benefits for others

You will inspire others and demonstrate best practice by making steady and assured progress towards a goal (rather than boom and bust). Fast progress looks exciting, but it doesn't last... we're after *sustainable* high performance. Others will not be negatively impacted by you failing to deliver on your commitments or requesting support at short notice.

Related habits

- Maximise value with minimal effort (habit 12)
- Manage your boundaries (habit 13)
- Work through the emotional change curve (habit 18)
- Speak your truth (habit 26)

Habit 25: Know You Always Have Four Choices

This habit reminds us that we are self-determined individuals forging our own futures day by day. We are always in control of our choices, regardless of what changes are happening around us at work, at home or in life. Whether we are deliberately initiating those changes, or they are being given 'to' us, knowing we always have choices can steady our nerves and strengthen our resolve.

#1 Change it – get involved and shape the outcome. This can be a good choice when there are big changes at work that will directly affect your role long term. Sometimes the people designing the changes do not have full information on how, or why, things are done the way they are at the moment and cannot fully assess the impact. Or there might be hurdles to implementing the proposed changes that they haven't anticipated, and which could derail the project. When you choose 'change it', you contribute to shaping the solution, or at least offer a constructive voice of resistance. Related habit 26, 'speak your truth'.

#2 Accept it. Decide to go with the flow. The change isn't important enough for you to resist or it's outside your control. For example: the way you submit your expenses has changed and you've got to learn a new process and update your software. You don't feel strongly about the change to resist it, as it doesn't affect much of your work. You set aside time to familiarise yourself with the new process and software. A non-work example: your relationship has ended because the other person no longer wants to be in a relationship with you. You've already tried couples counselling. Ultimately, they make their own choices and that is outside your control (habit 1, 'prioritise your sphere of control'). You'll have to find a way to emotionally let it go (habit 14, 'accept what is').

#3 Change me – reframe the situation until you can achieve personal alignment (habit 8). For example, the company is following a particular strategy, and you're not sure it's the right way to go. You've explained why, but the strategy remains the same, and you are not feeling aligned with the changes being proposed. If the change impacts you, and it's not something you can readily accept (choice #2), then it requires effort on your part to achieve personal alignment – when we are not aligned, we use considerable energy trying to resolve the internal tussle. One way to return to alignment is to reframe the change by looking for the silver lining and stick with it until you find at least three positive reasons to support the proposed way forward.

#4 Opt out. Leave the role/company/situation. Usually, you only make this choice if you've tried the first three options and you can't find a way to get into personal alignment about the change. The change is not something you can support so you decide to leave your role, the company, the relationship, the situation or the environment.

EXERCISE: PRACTICE MAKING YOUR FOUR CHOICES

Even if you are not actively wrestling with a major change at the moment, it can still be useful to work through your choices on a smaller scale so that when bigger changes do come along, and it's likely they will, you are already practised at the habit.

1. List a number of changes that are impacting you right now. For example, roadworks creating a diversion on your usual commute, a new process being implemented at work, a colleague is leaving so your role description will change to cover part of the role as well as your existing remit, you need to change your car.

2. Appraise the impact of each change. For example: is there a solution within your sphere of control or influence? Is it a small, medium or large disruption? Will the impact be short term or long term? What are the consequences of the change for you? Your family? What is the effort required on your part to 'change it', 'change me', 'accept it' or 'opt out'? What is the cost/ benefit of that effort?

3. Decide which of the four choices you are applying to each change, and why.

Benefits for you

Knowing you always have four choices gives you a sense of control and self-direction when it may feel as though change is being imposed upon you, rather than something you want to happen. You'll know that whatever happens, you will be all right.

Benefits for others

Seeing your example, others are inspired to make their own self-directed decisions rather than developing a mindset of being a victim of circumstance.

Related habits

- Prioritise your sphere of control (habit 1)
- Achieve personal alignment (habit 8)
- Accept what is (habit 14)
- Speak your truth (habit 26)

Habit 26: Speak Your Truth

One way we can feel more optimistic about the future is to speak up for ourselves if things are not going the way we hoped (see habit 13, 'manage your boundaries'), or if there's an opportunity we want to be considered for. Unless we speak up, we end up suffering in silence or voicing our desires / concerns to people who have no capacity to change the situation (usually our nearest and dearest). When we know what we want to say and we have the courage to voice it, we contribute to our sense of optimism because we are actively engaged in creating our future. Even if we don't get the outcome we want, we are emboldened by the fact that we spoke up and it is less daunting to do so again.

Rehearse what you want to say

To know what you want to say, you need to know what is not working for you or what you want the outcome to be. The more specific you can be, the easier it is for someone to help you. Is it a workload issue (see habit 24, 'bite off what you can chew'), an emotional moment (see habit 15, 'process emotions as data'), an alignment issue (see habit 8, 'achieve personal alignment'), something else (see habit 3, 'solve the root cause of the problem')? Can you illustrate with facts and specific examples?

If you are already implementing the resilience habits, and demands still feel overwhelming, sense-check with people you trust, so you have an idea of whether:

- You personally are 'off the pace' at the moment
- The demands being placed on you are unreasonable for anyone to deliver
- The demands are self-imposed and nobody else requires you to meet them

It's worth practising what you want to say by saying it out loud to yourself, because it forces you to find words to express your feelings. By saying it out loud, the thought is easier to evaluate as though someone else had said it. It's OK to test-drive what we want to say with people we trust before saying it to someone who can help us create a new reality. Can you anticipate the response from the person who can help you? What questions might they ask? Try to have your answers ready before you speak up so that you feel less pressured when you speak to them.

Gather your courage

Some people find it easier than others to start a difficult conversation. If you find it challenging to speak up, now would be a great time to review your happy file (see habit 23, 'create your happy file') to remind yourself that you are a resourceful and capable person with the right to be heard respectfully by others. You could also use habit 11, 'decide who is driving the bus') to bring forward your best persona for this situation. Or habit 8, 'achieve personal alignment' to feel more grounded.

Speak up

Once you know what you want to say, you need to speak up about what's on your mind or how you feel, even if it goes against the general flow of the discussion. Sometimes it takes courage in the moment to get the words out, and sometimes what you say is not as articulate as you'd hoped, but at least it's out. When you speak up, you add to the pool of shared information. Then a dialogue can begin, and both sides can share ideas to move the situation forward.

TOP TIPS: BREAKING INTO THE CONVERSATION

Try these phrases to encourage others to invite you to speak your truth:

- I have a different view
- That's not how I see it
- That doesn't work for me
- There's something else you haven't considered
- There are other options
- I'm not sure that's realistic

When you speak your truth, you will be more effective if you strike a balance between being passive or aggressive, ie assertive. This assertiveness includes your behaviour, the words you say and your body language:

	Passive	Assertive	Aggressive
Behaviour	Gives in to other people's requests straight away Refuses to ask for anything, even when it's necessary	States own needs, while respecting others' needs Firm about getting things done, rather than blaming Accepts mistakes and seeks solutions not scapegoats	Puts own needs first while ignoring or belittling other people's needs Patronising, sarcastic, blaming
Language	Uses phrases like 'sort of', 'try' or apologises frequently Avoids 'I' statements Speaks hesitantly, quietly, often leaving sentences unfinished	'I believe that... what do you think?' Offers positive suggestions Asks direct open questions Expresses feelings and requests plainly	'Just do it or else' Loud, strident voice Uses many 'I' statements Boasts about self Says 'should' and 'ought' Blames others
Body language	Moves about nervously Little eye contact Arms crossed in protection Fake smile when angry	Balanced, relaxed posture Steady gaze, but not a stare Moves hands expressively Looks angry when angry	Alert posture, directly facing you Too much eye contact, staring Finger-wagging or table-thumping Clenched jaw

Benefits for you

Whether your view is well received or not, you'll have more self-respect for honouring it and speaking up for yourself. You'll also have the opportunity to hear a validating point of view, or a contradictory one that may change your thinking. Speaking up also allows you to share a lesson learned despite a less than favourable outcome, which helps to inform your brand, rather than let others draw their own conclusions.

Benefits for others

When you speak up, you increase the pool of shared information, giving others an opportunity to consider a view that might not have occurred to them. If others hold a similar view but have not yet voiced it, your example may give them courage to speak up and echo your sentiment, which is particularly true when seeking to de-stigmatise conversations; for example, discussing mental health in the workplace.

Related habits

- Solve the root cause of the problem (habit 3)
- Achieve personal alignment (habit 8)
- Decide who is driving the bus (habit 11)
- Process emotions as data (habit 15)
- Create your happy file (habit 23)
- Bite off what you can chew (habit 24)

CHAPTER EIGHT

Meaning

M eaning, in this context, is used to describe both our
beliefs, how we make sense of events that happen to
us, and our purpose – why am I here?

Our beliefs are a lens through which we look at life and
determine the meaning we give to an event. Exploring,
through dialogue, the meaning behind someone acting in
a particular way can help us to see things from someone
else's perspective and show empathy. A teenager acting out,
from a parent's perspective might be given the meaning
that the teenager is being deliberately disruptive to make
you late for work as a protest for a curfew; the teenager
perspective might be that acting out is the only way to get
their parent's attention.

TIP: REFRAMING A NEGATIVE RESULT TO
REMAIN FOCUSED ON MOVING FORWARD

A smaller scale sense-making example that supports an optimistic outlook is to reframe things that didn't go to plan by looking for the silver lining. Stick with it until you find at least three positives. This helps you to consider how you interpret and respond to an event. For example, you missed your revenue target for the month. Silver lining 1 – you achieved 95% of target which was good considering it's out-of-season. Silver lining 2 – it keeps you and the team hungry for ways to improve – no room for complacency. Silver lining 3 – you'll have to demonstrate grit or creativity to get the results for the quarter back on track.

Finish the sentence 'Life is…'. For example, if your belief is 'Life is a battle', you'll apply that meaning to many of life's events creating a self-fulfilling prophecy, because your perception of life will be that there are many battles. If your belief is negatively phrased, try out a more empowering one. How would life be different if instead you thought 'Life is a gift' or 'Life is an adventure' or 'Life is a journey'? Given exactly the same event, what two people think about it would vary depending on their beliefs. The event didn't change, only the meaning they gave it. Pick whatever meaning works for you.

One way to uncover what is meaningful for you is to ask, 'What keeps me going when the going gets tough?'

Why it matters

Having a meaning gives us mental resilience in adversity. This is most powerfully explained by Viktor Frankl who, after surviving Auschwitz and other concentration camps, wrote a book called *Man's Search for Meaning*. One of my favourite quotes from the book is 'He who has a *why* can bear any *how*'. Frankl explains that if people suffer but see meaning in their life, they do not despair and are able to survive in spite of their suffering. People in the camp who had a strong why (for example, to return to their family or to have revenge on their captors) survived while others perished.

Fortunately, most of us will not be tested to such an extent. We can still recognise the principle that attributing meaning to an adverse event helps to strengthen our resolve. One example is maintaining cordial relations with your ex *for the sake of the children*. Meaning can also help us to make difficult decisions for the *greater good;* for example, announcing redundancies or being a whistle-blower. Meaning, along with your core values (see habit 8, 'achieve personal alignment') helps to inform your priorities.

This chapter includes the following habits:

27. Be kind to yourself – ensuring that your self-talk is positive and builds your confidence rather than being critical and discouraging.

28. Develop a growth mindset – the understanding that we can develop our abilities and intelligence to get better and achieve more.

29. Find your purpose – discovering why you do what you do, and how that keeps you going when the going gets tough.

30. Give back – offering your money, time or talents to benefit others has reciprocal benefit for your sense of perspective, growth and abundance.

Habit 27: Be Kind to Yourself

We all have a voice in our head; this is our self-talk, or our inner dialogue. That voice is mostly the result of social conditioning, unless we deliberately condition it. With a little practice, we can condition our self-talk to be positive and supportive.

> **EMPOWERING BELIEF**
> I am not my *thoughts*.

Let that idea settle in for a moment. Our thoughts are just that – thoughts. Some thoughts are echoes from those who influenced us in our childhood, and some are from the culture we grew up in. There may be some religious input, and there is definitely some school and work input: we've spent so long in those environments that the banter enters our thinking patterns without us realising it. As we each have such varied upbringings and live in different places, surrounded by different friends and family, even if we work at the same company, we have different inner dialogues. Maybe you're barely aware of your inner voice, maybe you're driven half mad by it wittering on, or – more likely – your awareness of it comes and goes over time.

- When you stop and notice your self-talk, what does it say? Do you recognise any dominant influencers? Parents? Teachers? Colleagues? Partners?
- When you stop and notice your self-talk, is it harsh or kind? Judgemental or generous? What is the general tone of your thoughts? Where did those thoughts originate?
- Under what circumstances does your inner critic show up more often?

If your self-talk is already kind and generous, that's great. You can speak to yourself as though you are someone you love, or as you would if you were giving feedback. For example, judge the action ('I did something stupid') not yourself ('I am stupid'). Take great care with words that follow 'I am…' as they resonate deeply with your identity.

If your inner critic is a bully, it is undermining your resilience all the time and you would benefit from sticking with this habit for the long haul. It may not be easy, as there's a lifetime of conditioning to wrestle with, but reconditioning your self-talk from being your worst enemy to your best friend and the resulting self-love is absolutely worth it. When we come to like who we are, we are no longer constantly wrestling with our inner critic and life seems so much sweeter. We have less fear and we can accomplish great things, not least in our relationships with others. After optimism, this habit is the one that is most life-changing because it improves all areas of your life.

EXERCISE: TAME YOUR INNER CRITIC

To start gaining control of your thoughts and making your self-talk positive, supportive and encouraging, try these steps:

1. Name your inner critic

Imagine your inner critic as a physical presence and describe it in detail. Make your description vivid and memorable.

- What does it look like?
- Is it big or small?
- Is it a recognisable thing or a presence?
- What colour is it?
- What would it be like to touch it?
- What does it smell like?
- What does it sound like?

Now give your inner critic a name. Use the first thing that pops into your head, no matter how ridiculous it sounds. You now have a mental handle on *a separate thing that is your inner critic... and not you.*

2. Be aware of your inner critic

Over the coming week, be aware of when your inner critic shows up.

- What types of things does it say?
- Is it helping or hindering you?

Sometimes our inner critic is pointing out possible obstacles and taking on a nurturing tone of 'concentrate' or 'pay attention', which may be helpful. In that case, a mental 'thank you, I've got it' respects your inner critic and lets you carry on with what you were doing. At other times, it might be berating, blaming or calling you names, hindering you from showing up as your best. Being aware of your self-talk is a great step forward.

3. Replace critical thoughts

Catch the unhelpful thoughts as they come up and replace them with a more compassionate version. For example, change 'You just don't get it' to 'You just don't get it, *yet*'. Better still, think of a kind and encouraging phrase that you heard as a child, or one that you say to others you nurture – something like 'You can do it, keep going'.

If you're in the middle of something and you can't spare the mental capacity to think of a direct replacement, having a phrase that's always available, for example, 'You can do it, keep going', can be useful. You could also offer a mental 'not now, you're not helping' to brush the thought aside. Often the voice comes back, but next time you may be able to do the replacement exercise.

Over time, your replacement phrases will become your default self-talk, so make them short, positive, personal, general and encouraging. '*You* (personal) *can* (positive) *do it* (general), *keep going* (encouraging)'. If in doubt, don't overthink it – think of an expression you'd say to a child to encourage them. Your own inner child will thank you.

'No amount of self-improvement can make up for any lack of self-acceptance.'
— Robert Holden, Psychologist

Psychologists, psychiatrists and psychotherapists have known for many years that our internal chatter affects our quality of life. In the last decade there have been significant advances in medical research; scientists can now provide measurable evidence that what we think (believe) affects the neural pathways in our brains and the chemical reactions in our bodies. Negative self-talk has a profound detrimental effect not only on your mental health, but also on your physical health. For an incredible read on using your mind to heal your body, I recommend Dr Joe Dispenza's book *You Are the Placebo (2014)*. He explains the science behind each link in the chain of causality that starts with a thought and ends with a biological fact.

The ability to literally change our mind at a biological level is called 'neuroplasticity'. In simple terms, if you have ever broken the arm you use most, you'll have been forced to use your other arm to compensate. Your brain quickly learns how to provide a similar level of dexterity to your non-dominant hand. If we 'injure' our inner critic and consistently replace those thoughts with kinder self-talk, eventually our kinder inner voice becomes stronger. But just as it would be easy to go back to using our dominant hand once it had healed, so too is it easy to revert to negative self-talk if we don't consciously choose more positive phrases. Changing our attitudes, beliefs, perceptions and behaviours takes time. Changing once is not enough. Self-mastery in this instance is making your self-talk an ongoing conscious choice.

When I discuss self-talk with coaching clients, they often validate negative chatter by saying 'It keeps me on my game' or 'I have high standards'. I used to say the same things. What I now know is that we can achieve that same drive from a place of self-love rather than strong critique. Learn to forgive (not forget) the hurtful events that created the initial drive and replace it with a higher purpose (habit 29, 'find your purpose') that serves others and that will require you to become the person it takes to it. Forgiveness is advanced work: a coach or counsellor will be able to help you if you aren't sure where to begin, or if you get stuck.

Benefits for you

Life is challenging enough without beating yourself up. You can achieve far more when you strive for ambitious goals that benefit others, beyond yourself and neutrally evaluate your performance towards those goals. With practice, you can learn to quickly adjust your stress hormones. When your inner critic starts blaming, your body starts releasing stress hormones. Replacing the chatter with kinder self-talk dampens the hormones again.

Benefits for others

Your inner critic becomes your outer critique of others, who will achieve less if they feel judged. Even if you believe that you give out a softer version of judgement than you apply to yourself, it will still be harsher than you think. When you acknowledge that you have no idea of the internal battles some people are waging it helps you show up with more compassion and seek first to understand their map of the world.

Related habits

- Accept what is (habit 14)
- Process emotions as data (habit 15)
- Avoid vicious cycles (habit 16)
- Develop a growth mindset (habit 28)
- Find your purpose (habit 29)

Habit 28: Develop a Growth Mindset

Carol Dweck, a professor at Stanford, popularised the term 'growth mindset' in her TED talk: 'The power of believing you can improve'. In her talk, she states that we have a growth mindset if we believe we can change and grow to improve ourselves and our capabilities, and we have a closed mindset if we believe we can't. As a trainer and educator, I consider growth mindset to be the essence of my craft.

We can encourage ourselves and others when we give the feedback 'not yet' instead of 'fail'. History books are crammed with examples of inventors who tried countless times to develop their ideas into fully fledged creations – two of the best known are Edison (and the light bulb) and Dyson (and the bagless vacuum cleaner). High achievers have tried and failed, and then learned and improved: no one comes out of the womb an expert.

A growth mindset is fundamental to our resilience because adversity is likely to challenge us in different ways at different times. If we have only one coping strategy, we are reducing our chances of having the right strategy for the circumstances. We can actively build our resilience toolkit by using the habits in this book. And if we have a background of being able to figure out new ways of doing things and adapting (that is, learning), we'll feel reassured that we'll find or make a way to overcome unexpected adversity, even if we don't yet know how. Sometimes extending our comfort zone is uncomfortable, but we also know that embracing the discomfort is necessary to advance and grow. By getting comfortable with being uncomfortable, knowing that we can grow, we build our optimism and ability to receive feedback gracefully.

Small consistent habits work best

The habits start to deliver benefits as you become proficient and use them regularly; much like cleaning your teeth, you don't get the full benefit if you only do it once! Psychologists used to believe it took twenty-one days to make or break a habit (Maltz, 1960), but with today's digital distractions, that figure has been updated to an average of sixty-six days to rewire our neural pathways to embed a new habit (Lally, 2009). So, if you're going to have to practice something that often it makes sense to start with only one to two small resilience habits and gradually add more to your toolkit once those are ingrained. A little patience and persistence is required. Trust the process.

Two months can feel like a long time to stay with a new habit, so my clients find that 3 × 21-day cycles, with a review every 21 days, works well.

Try it: the first 21 days provides a focus and the tenacity to develop a degree of proficiency in the habit and decide if the reward is worth the effort

Tune it: the second 21 days provides opportunity to fine tune the habit to something that suits you / your lifestyle better

Train it: the final 21 days often require less conscious effort and it's when you really lock in the new behaviour

Experiment to discover what works best for you.

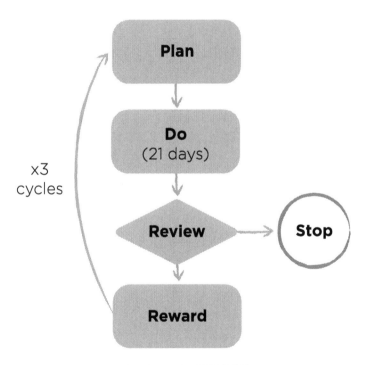

FIG. 8.1: EXPERIMENT CYCLE

EXERCISE: EXPERIMENT WITH A RESILIENCE HABIT

Use these questions to prompt you as you experiment with making a new resilience habit part of your daily practice.

Plan

- Which habit are you working on?

- What situations can you anticipate when this habit will help?

- How will you remind yourself to do this habit?

- What results will tell you that the new habit is working?

- What hurdles do you anticipate, and what's your contingency plan?

Do

- Stay alert to opportunities to use the new habit daily for 21 days.

- Consistency is important: aim for progress, not perfect.

- How will you hold yourself accountable?

Review

- Hold yourself accountable. Review your metrics.

- How often did you use your new habits?

- What benefits have you achieved?

- What do you need to tweak to get better results?

- Is it a habit you want to continue, or stop and try something else?

Reward

- Celebrate your progress so far on building your resilience. We all need rewards: the 'feel good' hormones associated with making progress help to sustain our momentum.

You can download a one-page template for planning your habit experiments from www.TheResilienceClub.co.uk

---

Over the years I have had to learn and relearn many of the resilience habits in this book. I still don't get it right every day, but I continue to get it right far more often than I get it wrong, and that's OK.

Benefits for you

By cultivating a growth mindset, you'll be open to new ideas, new experiences, diverse opinions and feedback, which often leads to high-quality conversations with like-minded others and builds your network. You'll have greater mental agility when faced with uncertainty, complexity or ambiguity and therefore be more inclined to solve the root cause of a problem rather than opt for a quick fix of a symptom. You'll also be more optimistic, because you feel more resourceful – you either know a way, or you'll discover one.

Benefits for others

When you have a growth mindset, you can better support others in developing a growth mindset and share with them useful resources you found through your own personal development and experience of learning.

Related habits

- Use role models and mentors (habit 6)
- Be kind to yourself (habit 27)

Habit 29: Find Your Purpose

This habit helps you to discover your purpose, the difference you want to make in the world. Unusually, for this habit only, I suggest that you complete the 'related habits' first. It's also likely that you'll develop this habit, and habit 9, 'shape your leadership identity' at the same time.

What impact do you want to have in the world? Why? At work, at home and in life. I'm not looking for answers like 'I'm good at it', 'to pay the bills' or 'because my parents did the same job'. I'm looking for a deeper answer to the question why that speaks of something beyond yourself: a greater good. It's a big question, and it might take some time for the answer to come to you, so I encourage you to enjoy the process of discovery. I do not advocate working on holiday. However, the discovery of your purpose does benefit from relaxed attention while you are taking a pause from day-to-day demands.

> **WHAT'S YOUR PURPOSE (OR LIVING LEGACY)?**
>
> What positive change (small or large) could you make in the world
>
> **– and witness it during your lifetime –**
>
> that will continue to have an impact long after you've died?

Find your purpose

Many of us are working daily towards something that will continue to exist after we depart this world: to raise children well, to further the body of knowledge in our field, to invent or create something, to be a role model in some way – there are countless ways to make the world a better place because we were in it. James Kerr's book *Legacy* (2013) about the New Zealand All Blacks, the most successful rugby team in history, powerfully explains the mindset: wearing an All Blacks shirt comes with a code of conduct described as 'our first responsibility is to be a good ancestor'.

The process of discovering your compelling purpose might prompt your internal critic to ask, 'Who do you think you are?' Imposter syndrome is a thinking pattern where you doubt your accomplishments and have a persistent fear of being exposed as a 'fraud', despite evidence of your competence. Overcoming imposter syndrome is greatly aided by positive self-talk and establishing your evidence base. Habit 27, 'be kind to yourself' and habit 23, 'create your happy file' are a good place to start.

EXERCISE: QUESTIONS TO UNCOVER YOUR PURPOSE

When you are feeling rested, positive and confident, ponder some, or all, of these questions and see what consistent theme develops.

1. What would a good friend write as your obituary?
2. What are you passionate about in a way that defines who you are?
3. Do your core values point to an overarching purpose in life?
4. What one thing do you think you are here for?
5. What would you do differently if you knew you had one year to live?
6. If you ruled the world and had unlimited resources, what would you change?
7. Who or what do you want to impact?
8. How do you want to instil change?

And finally, why is it important, *to you personally*, to have that impact?

Achieve professional alignment

The United Nations encourages businesses to align themselves with one of the seventeen global sustainability goals so that their collective efforts accelerate achievement of the greater good. Purpose-driven firms recognise people's desire for their work to have meaning; to attract the best candidates they include their purpose statement in their employee value proposition and embed it in the culture.

We tend to be good at what we love to do, because we willingly invest time in developing the related skills, knowledge and behaviours. Ideally, what you love to do can also earn you a living, and you are contributing those talents to your current role. A definition of work that is both paid and purposeful for you would sit at the intersection of these four standards:

1. What the world needs

2. What you love

3. What you are good at

4. What you can be paid for

EXERCISE: EVALUATING YOUR CURRENT WORK AGAINST YOUR PURPOSE

-   How well does your current role and employer satisfy your purpose (the four questions above)?

-   What would have to change to make it an even better fit? (habit 25, 'know you always have four choices')

    Change it – If your long-term career trajectory and life plans are aligned, but your talents and values are not, your current position may be a stepping stone that is taking you in the right direction. Can you redefine your role or contribution to be a better fit?

    Change me – Who can you talk to, to explore how your purpose aligns with the organisational purpose? If you can't find alignment, does your current position fulfil a different purpose? For example, to provide for your family?

Accept it – accept that your work is not aligned and find other avenues such as volunteering or a side-hustle to regularly participate in meaningful work.

Opt out – often a last resort, create an opportunity to follow your purpose that means leaving your current employer.

Share your purpose to increase your influence

Simon Sinek discusses meaning in terms of business purpose in his TEDx talk 'How Great Leaders Inspire Action'. He asserts that 'people don't buy what you do, they buy why you do it'. Having a clear purpose draws others to you. In times of change, leaders are meaning-makers. They help employees connect their personal meaning to a higher purpose to create belief and a sense of direction. For example, they explain the purpose behind organisational changes. When employees know what the ultimate goal of the change is, they can achieve personal alignment (or not) and make decisions that are in line with strategy without knowing the finer detail.

CASE STUDY: CREATING A VISION YOU PASSIONATELY BELIEVE IN

I was unsuccessful at my first attempt at a promotion board, but I was offered a second attempt in six months' time. During that period, I did the 'find your purpose' exercise. Although I am passionate about what I do I struggled to express it in words. I let ideas

> mull around in the background for a couple of weeks
> and then remembered an event that was emotive for
> me and captured the essence of why I do what I do.
> Reconnecting with that memory made it easier to explain:
> 'keeping people active across their lives and enjoying
> a prosperous environment... making things better for
> people'. The promotion board said that my strategic
> vision for the college was one of the best they'd seen,
> and I was promoted. I didn't have to 'sell' the vision, I was
> speaking from the heart.
>
> – Dr Chris Bussell, PVC Dean, College of Life and
>   Natural Sciences, University of Derby

Benefits for you

When your emotions and thinking are aligned with your moral compass, you feel a sense of grounded purpose. With purpose you elevate yourself to be bolder than you might otherwise have been. By creating stretch goals (habit 24, 'bite off what you can chew') that compel you to become a better version of yourself, you are more likely to remain committed to the end goal and not be easily disheartened by small diversions or failures along the way. You will have a 'living legacy', making a difference to others while you are still alive.

Knowing your 'why', your purpose, both supports and tests your resilience. It supports by providing a directional focus that remains steady when there is uncertainty all around. It provides the motivation for 'one more try' when you've had setback after setback. The pursuit of your purpose also tests your resilience by encouraging you beyond your comfort zone to become the person it takes to achieve such a lofty ambition.

When you are engaged in work you are good at and that has meaning for you, it is easier to achieve a sense of flow, that state where work is less effort, more enjoyable and achieves better results. Less effort is great for your resilience, as it demands less of you. In fact, it increases your sense of self-efficacy.

Benefits for others

If your bigger purpose is in service of others, they become your beneficiaries. For example, you are benefiting others indirectly if your purpose is to be someone who inspires others and who others choose to follow. Your team will benefit from your efforts to improve your management or leadership skills. You can also help others to find alignment between their purpose and that of the company.

Related habits

- Achieve personal alignment (habit 8)
- Shape your leadership identity (habit 9)
- Create your happy file (habit 23)
- Be kind to yourself (habit 27)
- Give back (habit 30)

Habit 30: Give Back

This habit is about volunteering your time and skills to do something for those less fortunate than yourself. Maybe you already embrace the spirit of giving by helping neighbours, family, friends or schools on an ad-hoc basis as part of an extended community. Also spare a thought, or your money, time and talents, for those who don't have someone looking out for them. We can all benefit from knowing that someone cares about us and will support us if we fall.

If you haven't volunteered before, it may not be immediately obvious how giving to others in this way helps you to develop your resilience. *In Leading for a Lifetime (Bennis and Thomas, 2007)* the authors identify three qualities of outstanding leaders. One of these is 'adaptive capacity' – the ability to learn about yourself, the world around you and what it takes to change yourself or others. One way to create stretch zone opportunities that develop your adaptive capacity and growth mindset is to use your skills and talents in a new environment – maybe paid or through volunteering. A more obvious cognitive benefit is that it provides a sense of perspective on the things that are troubling you, which may seem less pressing after a day of working to support those in less fortunate circumstances. Volunteering can also be a way to feel deeply fulfilled by doing work that is meaningful for you, supporting a cause you believe in. I believe in unconditional giving, that we give with no expectation of receiving, and yet it's undeniable that when we give, we also receive. Humans are tribal by nature, and our biochemistry seeks to reinforce community-centric behaviour. When we help others, our body generates oxytocin, the 'hug drug', which makes us feel good about what we do to support others.

I am passionate about learning and enabling everyone to be the best they can be. I was previously a Girlguide leader and now organise and participate on behalf of The Human Library™. What good causes resonate with you? Start with the top tips and get involved, for their sake and yours.

TOP TIPS: EXAMPLES OF NON-MONETARY WAYS TO GIVE BACK

- Service: help at your local charity shop, a roundtable event, a Christmas soup kitchen, a company-organised event for a specific charity, be a responsible adult for the scouting movement, join a mountain rescue team, or help remove graffiti. If you prefer not to be 'front-of-house', get involved 'back-of-house'; for example, collecting, sorting, promoting, organising or advocating for a charity.
- Connection: join one of the befriending services tackling loneliness, volunteer as a listener for the Samaritans, become a mental health first aider at work, support a community for under-represented groups.
- Gifts: leave the extras from your vegetable patch by the gate with a sign saying, 'help yourself', plant trees or donate unwanted items to charity.
- The Human Library™ is designed to build a positive framework for conversations that can challenge stereotypes and prejudices through dialogue. The

> Human Library™ is a place where real people are on loan to readers, a place where difficult questions are expected, appreciated and answered. A worldwide movement for social change. Don't judge a book by its cover. Watch the video – Creating The Human Library: Fighting taboos & stigma through dialogue by Ronni Abergel, TEDxBucharest.

If you don't currently have the capacity to offer your time and skills perhaps you could contribute financially to worthy causes? Traditionally people offered a tithe, 10% of their income. Many of us give financial donations to worthy causes or sponsor our friends and family. If you do this, please continue. Your regular direct debit will help their cause and, *if you do it consciously*, you'll get a warm feeling from knowing that you can, and do, support those less fortunate than yourself.

Small businesses can get connected to a movement called B1G1: Business for Good. The idea of buy-one-give-one is that lots of small giving impacts make a difference; for example, every time a coffee shop sells a cup of coffee, they give access to life-saving water to those who really need it. When you're part of B1G1, you bring new purpose, meaning and relevance in your business by embedding giving right at the core of what you do. With B1G1, more than 2,300 businesses from 43 countries have made 150+ million impacts: www.b1g1.com.

Benefits for you

It feels good to help others. It reminds you of gratitude and humility, increases your sense of abundance, and enables you to develop new or existing skills in a different environment. It challenges, confirms or informs your core values, broadens your social network, provides opportunity to develop your emotional self-management and stimulates different ways of thinking.

Benefits for others

Whether it's a regular commitment, or random acts of kindness, giving back provides others with greater resources or emotional benefits.

Related habits

- Create magic moments (habit 22)
- Develop a growth mindset (habit 28)
- Find your purpose (habit 29)

Summary

I define resilience as the ability to take the challenges and changes of life in your stride and to say 'yes' to the opportunities that excite you.

While the *trigger* of the stress might be outside your control, how you *perceive* the stress and how you *respond* to it are within your control.

When you are operating within healthy stress limits, your contribution is effective, your energy is high, and your outlook is positive. But if something upsets the picture, you can become a candidate for burnout. Your intuition and your body alert you to the fact that you are overdoing it, if you listen. Acknowledging the symptoms early makes for a swifter remedy.

Your capacity to serve others is directly linked to how well you look after yourself.

Proactively building your resilience habits can increase your capacity to take on more challenges, reduce existing stress and prepare you for unexpected adversity.

The FREEDOM model contains thirty powerful habits that help you invest in yourself as a whole person: mind, body, spirit and emotions. You've dipped into the habits in the main part of the book as the need arose, and you have, or are working towards, a balance of resilience habits across the seven categories. You've discovered that the habits are entirely within your control, simple to understand, quick to do, can be done anywhere, cost no money and require no kit. You know the solutions are practical, frequent and free, and the only barrier to progress is your willingness to act on what you know. You have likely proven to yourself that you can improve your resilience by making small daily lifestyle changes, whatever the many and varied demands on your time and energy. You understand that investing in your resilience will give you huge returns in the long term – and you also get to enjoy the benefits now. You also appreciate that developing your resilience is an ongoing practice. It's unlikely that you'll slip back into old ways that don't serve you, but if you do, you'll spot it early and be able to get back on track.

Working on the habits in this book will help you cultivate the belief that 'whatever happens, I will be all right'. You'll experience greater control and feel energised by doing the things that make you feel like *you*, which is important because when we feel truly alive, we are a delight to be around, we add more value at work, we are more present as parents, and we do more to enrich the lives of those around us. Have you noticed the influence you'll be having on the people around you who are following your lead on self-care so that they too can think, act and behave from a place of being fully resourced?

Keep up the good work and you'll remain healthy, sane and in good spirits whatever comes your way.

Get in touch

This book will evolve as the workplace changes. If you come across any mistakes, if you know of other, better habits, if you have suggestions of how a habit can be further developed, or if you simply want to make a comment, please email me. You can find my contact details at www .AngelaArmstrong.com

I wish you all the best with sustaining your high performance, and I hope you now feel equipped to make an even bigger difference in the world and live life to the full while you do it.

You can access free resources to help you increase your resilience by visiting www.TheResilienceClub.co.uk. If you want to ask me for more advice about resilience, change or leadership, or share a success case study from using these habits, please get in touch.

🌐 www.AngelaArmstrong.com
in www.linkedin.com/in/AngelaKArmstrong

APPENDICES

Stress Triggers

Top ten stress triggers for each environment.

Life

1. Death of a spouse

2. Imprisonment

3. Death of a close family member

4. Immediate family member taking their own life

5. Getting into debt that you can't repay

6. Being homeless

7. Immediate family member being seriously ill

8. Unemployment (of main breadwinner)

9. Divorce

10. Break-up of family

Workplace

1. Poor management
2. Excessive workload
3. Unrealistic targets
4. Not enough support from managers
5. Job insecurity
6. Reduction in budgets
7. Bad workplace atmosphere
8. Not enough support from colleagues
9. Threat of redundancy or change
10. Friction with other staff

Entrepreneur

1. Expectations (of self, family and friends)
2. Cash flow
3. Closure-frustration (too many part-finished tasks)
4. Excessive workload
5. Lack of access to finance or other support
6. Staffing issues (especially business partner)
7. Competition
8. Legal challenge or insolvency
9. Unable to 'switch off'
10. Loneliness

Symptoms of Burnout

Here's a small selection of burnout symptoms based on my own experience, that of colleagues, and the excellent book *The Joy of Burnout* by Glouberman (2003). They are not a medical definition. Burnout is not recognised as a distinct medical disorder because it is problematically close to depressive disorders. If any resonate with you, it could be time to take action.

Sick and tired

- Work is not pleasurable
- Your to-do list never ends, but you're the only one who can do the tasks
- Your stress levels have gone through the roof
- You fear everything will fall apart if you stop
- You worry, hate, get tearful or are cynical more than usual
- You've started getting ill, but you used to be healthy

Burning out

- You no longer enjoy things that used to give you pleasure
- You are putting in more effort than usual but achieving less
- Your self-confidence is waning
- Everyone else seems to be operating on a slower speed setting to you
- You forget things or find yourself staring into space
- You want to get off the treadmill, there's too much to do.

Burned out

- You don't know what you're doing it all for
- You feel emotionally detached from everything
- You feel that nothing you do makes a difference anyway
- You're tired of taking care of everything and everyone, but you can't stop
- You're exhausted from the moment you wake up
- The thought of being seriously ill makes you think at least you'll get some rest

Examples of Core Values

Accountability	Dignity	Involvement	Responsibility
Achievement	Diversity	Justice	Results
Adaptability	Empathy	Knowledge	Reverence
Advancement	Energy	Leadership	Risk-taking
Adventure	Enthusiasm	Learning	Safety
Attentiveness	Entrepreneurship	Listening	Security
Authority	Environment	Long-term view	Service
Balance	Ethics	Love	Socialising
Being the Best	Fairness	Loyalty	Spirituality
Belonging	Faith	Money	Stamina
Caring	Family	Opportunities	Status
Caution	Focus	Organisation	Success
Challenge	Forgiveness	Partnering	Teamwork
Collaboration	Friendship	Peace	Tolerance
Collegiality	Honesty	Positivity	Tradition
Community	Humour/Fun	Power	Trust

Compassion	Impact	Prestige	Unity
Competition	Improvement	Productivity	Variety
Confidence	Independence	Profit	Vision
Contribution	Influence	Purpose	Wealth
Control	Initiative	Quality	Winning
Cooperation	Innovation	Recognition	Wisdom
Creativity	Integrity	Resilience	
Customer	Intelligence	Respect	

List of Words for Emotions

Based in part on Plutchik (1991)

Amused	Hopeful	Respected
Appreciated	Important	Responsive
Cheerful	Joyful	Secure
Confident	Loving	Serene
Content	Nurturing	Successful
Creative	Optimistic	Surprised
Daring	Peaceful	Thankful
Energetic	Playful	Thoughtful
Excited	Powerful	Trusting
Faithful	Proud	Valuable
Fascinating	Relaxed	Worthwhile

Angry	Guilty	Mad
Anxious	Hateful	Overwhelmed
Apathetic	Helpless	Rejected
Bored	Hurt	Sad
Confused	Inadequate	Sarcastic
Critical	Inferior	Scared
Depressed	Insecure	Selfish
Discouraged	Insignificant	Sceptical
Distant	Isolated	Sleepy
Embarrassed	Jealous	Stupid
Frustrated	Lonely	Tired

Bibliography

Bandler, R. and Grinder, J. (1990) *Frogs into Princes: Introduction to Neurolinguistic Programming.* Eden Grove Editions.

Barnes, D., Yaffe, K., Byers, A., McCormick, M., Schaefer, C., Whitmer, R. (2012) *Midlife vs late-life depressive symptoms and risk of dementia: differential effects for Alzheimer disease and vascular dementia.* Arch Gen Psychiatry. 69(5): 493–498. www.ncbi.nlm.nih.gov/pmc /articles/PMC3704214

Bennis, W. and Thomas, R. (2007) *Leading for a Lifetime: How Defining Moments Shape Leaders of Today and Tomorrow.* Harvard Business Review Press. Brighton.

Bhagat, S., Burke, M., Diuk, C., Filiz, I., Edunov, S. (2016) Three and a half degrees of separation, Facebook research

blog. https://research.fb.com/three-and-a-half-degrees-of
-separation [Accessed 13.3.19]

Brown, B. (2015) *Rising Strong: If we are brave enough, often enough, we will fall. This is a book about getting back up.* Penguin Random House. London.

Brown, B. (2010) The Gifts of Imperfection: *Let Go of Who You Think You're Supposed to Be and Embrace Who You Are.* Hazelden FIRM. Center City, Minnesota.

Cardia, H. and Miralles, F. (2017) *Ikigai: The Japanese Secret to a Long and Happy Life.* Hutchinson. London.

Cashman, K. (2018) *Leadership from the Inside Out: Becoming a leader for life.* Berrett-Koehler Publishers. Oakland.

Chapman, G. (2015) *The 5 love languages – the secret to love that lasts.* Moody Publishers. Chicago.

Chapman and White (2012) – *The 5 Languages of Appreciation in the Workplace – Empowering organisations by encouraging people.* Moody Publishers. Chicago.

Clark, N. *et al (2017) Professional Services Leadership Handbook: How to Lead a Professional Services Firm in a New Age of Competitive Disruption.* Kogan Page. New York.

Covey, S.R. *(2004) The 7 Habits of Highly Effective People: Powerful Lessons in Personal Change.* Simon & Schuster. London.

Csikszentmihalyi, M. (2002) *Flow: The Classic Work on How to Achieve Happiness*. Random House Group. London.

Dannemiller, K.D., and Jacobs, R.W. (1992) Changing the way organizations change: a revolution of common sense. *Journal of Applied Behavioral Science*, 28(4), 480–498.

Dispenza, J. (2014) *You Are the Placebo: Making your Mind Matter*. Hay House. London.

Dweck, C.S. (2017) *Mindset – Updated Edition: Changing the Way You Think to Fulfil Your Potential*. Ballantine Books. New York.

Dweck, C. (2014) TED Talk: *The power of believing that you can improve* www.ted.com/talks/carol_dweck_the_power _of_believing_that_you_can_improve?language=en [Accessed 13.03.2019]

Frankl, V. (2011) *Mans Search for Meaning: The Classic Tribute to Hope from the Holocaust*. Rider. London.

George, B. *(2015) Discover Your True North: Becoming an Authentic Leader*. John Wiley & Sons. New Jersey.

Gimson, A., Schlosser, M., Huntley, J.D., et al. (2018) *Support for midlife anxiety diagnosis as an independent risk factor for dementia: a systematic review*. British Medical Journal Open 8:e019399. doi:10.1136/ bmjopen-2017-019399 https://bmjopen.bmj.com/content /bmjopen/8/4/e019399.full.pdf

Goleman, D. (1996) *Emotional Intelligence: Why it can matter more than IQ. Bloomsbury Publishing. London.*

Harvard Medical School (2011) Understanding the stress response: chronic activation of this survival mechanism impairs health. [Blog post] www.health.harvard.edu/staying -healthy/understanding-the-stress-response [Accessed 25 November 2018].

Jennison, J. (2018) *Leading Through Uncertainty: Emotional Resilience and Human Connection in a Performance-Driven World.* Practical Inspiration Publishing. Basingstoke.

Katie, B. (2002) Loving What Is: Four Questions that Can Change Your Life. Random House Group. London.

Kerr, J. (2013) *Legacy: What the All Blacks Can Teach Us About the Business of Life.* Constable. London.

Koch, R. (2014) Living the 80/20 Way: Work Less, Worry Less, Succeed More, Enjoy More. Nicholas Brealey. London.

Kotter, J. (2012) *Leading Change. Harvard Business Review Press. Boston.*

Kotter, J. (2012) The Heart of Change: Real-Life Stories of How People Change Their Organizations. Harvard Business Review Press. Boston.

Kubler-Ross, E., and Kessler, D. (2014) On Grief and Grieving: Finding the Meaning of Grief Through the Five Stages of Loss. Simon & Schuster. London.

Krogerus, M. and Tschäppeler, R. (2017) *The Decision Book: Fifty models for strategic thinking*. Profile Books. London.

Lally, P., Potts, H., van Jaarsveld, C., and Wardle, J. (2010) 'How are habits formed: modelling habit formation in the real world'. *European Journal of Social Psychology*, 40(6), 998–1009.

Maltz, M. (2016) *Psycho-Cybernetics, A New Way to Get More Living Out of Life*. Tarcher Perigree. New York.

Mariotti A. (2015). The effects of chronic stress on health: new insights into the molecular mechanisms of brain-body communication. Future science OA, 1(3), FSO23. doi:10.4155/fso.15.21 https://www.ncbi.nlm.nih.gov/pmc/articles/PMC5137920

Patterson, K., Grenny, J., Mcmillan, R. and Switzler, A. (2011). *Crucial conversations: tools for talking when stakes are high*. McGraw-Hill.

Plutchik, R. (1991) *The Emotions*. University Press of America. New York.

Rotter, J.B. (1966) 'Generalized expectancies for internal versus external control of reinforcement'. *Psychological Monographs: General and Applied*, 80, 1–28.

Scott, K.A., Melhorn, S.J., & Sakai, R.R. (2012). *Effects of Chronic Social Stress on Obesity*. Current obesity reports, 1(1), 16–25 www.ncbi.nlm.nih.gov/pmc/articles/PMC3428710

Scouller, J. (2016) *The Three Levels of Leadership: How to Develop Your Leadership Presence, Knowhow and Skill* (2nd edition). Management Books. Oxford.

Alex Sheen, TEDx, Because I said I would https://www .youtube.com/watch?v=Iooz1TrCmbs [Accessed 17.3.19]

Southwick, S.M., and Charney, D.S. (2018) *Resilience: The Science of Mastering Life's Greatest Challenges*. Cambridge University Press. Cambridge.

Townsend, H. and Larbie, J. (2016) *How to Make Partner and Still Have a Life: The Smart Way to Get to the Top and Stay at the Top*. Kogan Page. London.

Thomas, R. (2008) *Crucibles of Leadership: How to Learn from Experience to Become a Great Leader*. Harvard Business Press. Boston.

Valdes-Dapena, C. (2018) *Lessons from Mars: How One Global Company Cracked the Code on High Performance Collaboration and Teamwork*. Change Makers Books. Winchester.

Williams, S. and Cooper, C. (1998) 'Measuring Occupational Stress: Development of the Pressure Management Indicator'. *Journal of Occupational Health Psychology* (Vol 3. No. 4. 306–321)

Useful Resources

Materials to support you in applying the habits in this book are available at www.TheResilienceClub.co.uk. You can also download a sample chapter.

Foundations of energy such as: sleep, hydration, nutrition and movement

- Walker, M. (2018) *Why We Sleep: The New Science of Sleep and Dreams*. Scribner Book Company. New York.

- Chatterjee, R. (2018) *The Four Pillar Plan: How to Relax, Eat, Move, Sleep Your Way to a Longer Healthier Life.* Penguin Life. UK.

- Chatterjee, R. (2018) *The Stress Solution: The 4 Steps to Reset Your Body, Mind, Relationships & Purpose.* Penguin Life. UK.

- Glouberman, D. (2003) *The Joy of Burnout: How burning out unlocks the way to a better, brighter future.* Hodder Stoughton. London.

Solve the root cause: Managing your finances

- Callaghan, G. et al. (2007) *Personal Finance.* John Wiley & Sons. Chichester.
- Eker, T (2007) *Secrets of the Millionaire Mind: Think Rich to Get Rich.* Piatkus. London.
- Wilson, A. (2014) *The Wealth Chef: Recipes to Make your Money Work Hard So You Don't Have To.* Hay House. London.

Solve the root cause: Strong relationships

- Armstrong, Alison (2013) *The Queen's Code.* PAX Programs Incorporated. Sherman Oaks, California.
- Deida, D. (2004) *The Way of the Superior Man: A Spiritual Guide to Mastering the Challenges of Women, Work and Sexual Desire.* Sounds True. Boulder.
- Heller, R. and Levine, A. (2012) *Attached: The New Science of Adult Attachment and How it Can Help You Find – and Keep – Love.* Jeremy P. Tarcher

Acknowledgements

Life is a collaboration, and this book was made possible with the support of many wonderful people who have been generous in sharing their time and energy with me.

To nanny Vera, the Queen of Resilience, you are an inspiration and I love you to bits.

To Dad, for all our late nights, gritty conversations, long walks, hard truths and holding each other in our process until it was done, and only then... big hugs. I love that you see both the strength and gentleness in me, as I do you. I love you.

To granddad Jack, Kathleen and Pop, for showing me through your example what it means to be a force for good. To Gary, for lighting a fire in my spirit that is unquenchable. I walk every day with the strength of my ancestors.

Tony Bickerstaff, thank you for offering a CFO perspective, your candour, and for role-modelling resilient leadership.

To the decision-makers who hired me to deliver resilience workshops and leadership programmes: thank you for working towards creating a culture of sustainable high performance in which people can thrive and do their best work.

A big thank you to all my workshop delegates and coaching clients who have tried and tested all the habits in this book and provided feedback on the results you have achieved. You trusted me even when you were sceptical, and you stuck with it to get the results. I salute you – you reaffirm my passion for this work and fill my heart with every success you have. A particular thank you to Ian Black, James Bulleid, Dr Chris Bussell, Carrie Caladine, Akram Habib, Karan Johal, Mike Simpson and Fiona Shelton for sharing your stories.

To Daniel Priestley and the Key Person of Influence programme, for providing actionable insights and a high-quality peer group who inspired me to turn 'I'm going to write a book one day' into 'I'm a published author'. Onwards and upwards.

To Joe Gregory, Kate Latham, Laura Ripper, Lucy McCarraher and Anke Ueberberg at Rethink Press, Michelle Abrahall (for illustrations) and Paul Jennings (for book cover inspiration) thank you for adding your individual expertise to get this book from first draft to published and looking so professional.

To Alison Jones for believing in me and this business book at the proposal stage. Your insights in the early days were invaluable. To my street team, for reviewing and commenting on the early drafts and for general cheering from the side-lines: Naeem Arif, Michelle Baden-Daintree, Lyn Bromley, Brian Chaplin, Vikki Coombes, Annette Gann, Stuart Hemming, David Hopkins, Liz Katz, Renford Marsden, Grace Marshall, Jaime Maxwell-Grant, Julie Meeson, Anna Molony, Gemma Rees, Helen Routledge, Ian Shreeve and Anne Taylor.

A special mention to Jude Jennison and Okokon Udo for calling me forth to be my highest self, encouraging me to speak my truth, and your unwavering support.

A big thank you to Andrew and Gill, the owners of the remote cottage where I did the majority of my writing, for bringing me a steady supply of logs and delicious home-cooked meals so that I could remain in flow.

And last but not least, my thanks to Mike Byrne, Emma Cooper and Louise Seymour for leaning in to the hard conversations about burnout way back when, and for nudging me back on track. You made more of a difference than you'll ever know.

Thank you everyone, here's to the next book!

The Author

Angela Armstrong PhD is a strategic leadership partner helping senior leaders within professional services to deliver sustainable high performance. She is an author, leadership specialist and learning consultant. A business owner since 2013, Angela previously worked at Accenture, a global management consultancy firm, where she led national transformation programmes. In 2010 she burned out and bounced back. Having shared her burnout story on the TEDx stage she was asked by her leadership delegates to write a book of resilience habits. Angela works with executives, senior leaders and owners of fast-growth businesses to develop leaders who deliver sustainable high performance. She gets fast results that last, new clients often start with a 2.5-hour resilience masterclass that turns 'knowing into doing', a full day resilience workshop or inviting Angela to speak at events. Her leadership-development programme equips leaders with the mindset, skill set and behaviours necessary to deliver commercial results and evolve their firm's products and services... without breaking themselves, the business, or their people in the process.

Angela loves to travel and is a keen dancer, she lives in Warwickshire, UK, and works internationally, via voice/video calls, and in person.

www.AngelaArmstrong.com

TEDx Talk 'How to Solve the Stress Epidemic'

26291285R00151

Printed in Great Britain
by Amazon